the
vegan
baker

More than 50 delicious recipes for vegan-friendly cakes, cookies, bars and other baked treats

Dunja Gulin

photography by
Clare Winfield

LONDON • NEW YORK

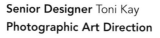

Senior Designer Toni Kay
Photographic Art Direction
   Megan Smith and Iona Hoyle
Commissioning Editor
   Céline Hughes
Production Toby Marshall
Editorial Director Julia Charles
Art Director Leslie Harrington
Prop Stylists Jo Harris and
   Liz Belton
Food Stylist Lucy Williams
Indexer Hilary Bird

First published in the UK in 2013
by Ryland Peters & Small
20–21 Jockey's Fields
London WC1R 4BW
and
519 Broadway, 5th Floor
New York, NY 10012
www.rylandpeters.com

10 9 8 7 6 5 4 3 2 1

Text © Dunja Gulin 2013
Design and photographs
© Ryland Peters & Small 2013

ISBN: 978-1-84975-351-7

A CIP record for this book is
available from the British Library.

A CIP record for this book is
available from the Library of
Congress

Printed in China

notes

• All spoon measurements are level unless otherwise specified.

• Ovens should be preheated to the specified temperature. Recipes in this book were tested using a regular oven. If using a fan-assisted/convection oven, follow the manufacturer's instructions for adjusting temperatures.

• When a recipe calls for the grated zest of citrus fruit, buy unwaxed fruit and wash well before use. If you can only find treated fruit, scrub well in warm soapy water and rinse before using.

Contents

Introduction

Baking: it has always been a magical word for me. Sweet baking was, and still is, even more magical, and I think many people will understand what I'm saying! The smell of freshly baked crescent rolls my nonna used to make for Christmas is one of the few things I can remember from my early childhood.

Maybe that's why my first attempts in the kitchen were baking simple cakes, learning how to flip pancakes and burning batch after batch of cookies. But I never gave up.

At high school, I decided to stop eating meat, and later when I left home to study I decided to try eating more vegan food after sampling so many of the disastrous 'vegetarian' dishes we were offered in student canteens. Back then, finding a vegan dessert that wasn't either a brick or a mass of soggy gruel was next to impossible, especially on a student budget. Also, I adored desserts and had no intention of giving them up! So, I decided to take my sweet-tooth destiny into my own hands and start some serious vegan baking!

It wasn't easy. Like everything else in life, you have to work hard. As with most 'conventional baking', vegan baking has quite a lot of specific rules that you have to follow without exception. I feel that, in some cases, it has more in common with chemistry than it does with intuitive cooking! But, what I love about it is the unpredictability, the excitement, the anticipation and the burst of joy that one feels when an experiment bakes into a tasty and beautiful thing! And I'm lucky enough to have the opportunity to share some of my discoveries with the world. I feel honoured.

There are various possible reasons why you decided to give this book a try. You might be fed up with the heavy feeling in your stomach after eating a regular dessert. You might be allergic to dairy or eggs but don't want to miss out on eating tasty desserts. You could be vegan for ethical reasons and your new year's resolution is to test your talent in baking. Maybe you want to lose weight, or you might just be curious to see how on earth you can bake a delicious dessert with 'nothing'…

Well, let me tell you, this 'nothing' that I use in making cakes are actually so many, so delicious and so healthy that the list will leave you speechless!

The reason I would encourage every person on this planet – whether vegan or not – to enjoy vegan desserts is the feeling you have after eating a healthy, natural dish that is not loaded with eggs, milk and sugar. Even though I don't have anything against these ingredients being eaten occasionally (in fact I do object to milk and sugar, but that's another story), when they are combined in a single dish, and especially when refined flour is used as well, they are quite harmful to the body, and can result in health problems in the long term.

However, taking any regime to extremes, vegan included, won't do much good for your health or mental wellbeing. What I've noticed is that many vegan baking books are guided by one rule – all the recipes have to be vegan. That means they are still full of refined sugar, margarine, highly refined flour and other processed vegan ingredients. So, you opt for not eating any animal products, but you might also put yourself on the path to becoming an unhealthy vegan.

That is why, when testing baking recipes, I am guided by more rules than one. I want my vegan cakes to be healthy; I want them to be made with the best ingredients I can afford; I want them to be organic whenever possible; sweet but not overly sweet; visually appealing but not fussy; perfect in their imperfections; I want them to feed my body; and I want them to feed my soul. These are my eight golden rules. If most of them are met, the result will be a gorgeous homemade cake that no one will ever say 'no' to. Try and you'll see!

Now let's look at the ingredients used in healthy vegan baking, my way.

Essential vegan baking ingredients

Flours

As the essential ingredient in baking, flour makes a big difference in successful dessert-making so carefully choose the best kind available. Buy organic brands that are unbleached and not treated with chemicals. Store them in airtight containers to prevent bugs and moths having a feast. Do not substitute plain/all-purpose flour for wholemeal/whole-wheat flour if not stated in the recipe, as the latter has more bran and is heavier both in structure and taste. Quality and protein percentages vary from brand to brand and from season to season. This might result in baking problems and, even if the recipe works really well once, there is no guarantee it will work so well next time if you are using a different brand of flour. Don't get scared! I'll talk more about this in the troubleshooting section on pages 16–17.

Unbleached plain/all-purpose flour

I use this type of flour most often since it makes a great base for almost any flour combination, and I would recommend using at least 60% of this type of flour in cake mixtures and bread dough to get a good texture and rise. It can be replaced with unbleached spelt flour if you prefer spelt to wheat. In emergencies, you can use bleached flour instead.

Wholemeal/whole-wheat flour

Robust and full-flavoured, wholemeal/whole-wheat flour contains – besides starch and protein – vitamins, fibre and minerals from the wheat's bran and germ. It has a shorter shelf-life, which is a good sign, but moths love it, so keep it tightly stored. If you live in a hot climate, keep it refrigerated. In baking, using entirely wholemeal/whole-wheat flour usually results in a heavy, dense and nutty texture and flavour which isn't usually what we want for a cake. A small percentage (up to 15%) added to the unbleached flour, however, will give a great texture and add flavour to any cake mixture or dough.

Fine cornmeal

There seems to be some confusion between the terms cornflour, cornmeal and cornstarch in British and American English. By cornmeal I mean yellow flour made out of dried corn kernels that is finely ground and used in baking, mixed with other flours. It should not be very coarse (like polenta) and it should not be a completely white powder (like cornflour/cornstarch). Cornmeal is quite heavy and dense, so I never use it on its own. It makes lovely sweet-tasting breads and gives a nice yellow colour to pie and tart crusts. Cornflour/cornstarch is used as a thickener (see page 15).

Other flours and grain products

There are always a couple more types of flour and grain products stored in my cupboard, waiting to be used. *Spelt flour* is nice to have for variety and when you wish to lessen the gluten content in baking. Sometimes a dough might ask for more protein, for example in bread, so having *strong/bread flour* is also good. *Chestnut flour* is a treat and I use it for special occasions to make delicious Castagnaccio (page 32). *Semolina/farina* is a type of ground wheat, completely white and mostly used to make semolina pudding, not as a flour. But I found some interesting ways for using it in baking and I hope you will like the taste and texture of those desserts as much as I do!

Couscous is also a wheat product, more coarsely ground than semolina, and yellowish in colour. It gives a great crunch to cookies!

Filo/phyllo pastry are paper-thin sheets made out of flour and water and used for making all kinds of baked delicacies, especially in Middle Eastern and Balkan cuisines. My baking is somewhat influenced by the latter, so you will find a couple of interesting, exotic and very tasty desserts made with this dough. Don't be afraid of it and try each filo/phyllo recipe at least once – you'll be surprised how tasty and easy they are!

Clockwise from top left
chestnut flour, wholemeal/whole-wheat flour, unbleached plain/all-purpose flour, couscous, cornmeal

Left to right

agave syrup, maple syrup, brown rice syrup, barley malt, Demerara sugar

Sweeteners

How to make desserts sweet and still be classed as healthy is one of the great mysteries. It can be done, but any answer I or some other cookbook author offers will probably be a potential topic for debate. What I have realized is that, especially in the United States, one healthy sweetener takes the throne and is revered until a controversy breaks out and another, 'healthier' sweetener takes the stage, then another and so on. In my opinion, the truth lies somewhere in between.

We all know processed foods are not good for us. At all. White sugar is one of the most refined foods available, and I never ever use it in my kitchen and avoid eating any food that contains it. This is not easy, as processed sugar is hiding everywhere; peeping from every can, every jar and every bread basket!

The sweeteners that I'm suggesting are the ones available to me and those that I have tested over the years, paying attention to how I felt after eating desserts sweetened with these rather than highly refined sugar. I have become quite sensitive to refined sugar over time and feel hot, restless and unfocussed when I eat it. I encourage you to test my method and see the difference for yourself: stop eating anything with refined sugar for a period of 30 days and then 'treat' yourself with a piece of your usual sugary cake. You should notice the bitter taste that sugary creams have and how afterwards your mouth feels weird and you need to brush your teeth immediately. For me, sugar acts like a mild poison, and I feel happy to have realized that early enough in life to stop my sugar addiction. That's right, eating sugar becomes an addiction; it's a relatively new addiction that is socially acceptable and encouraged by the media. It's a gazillion-dollar business that throws people into diabetes, obesity, high blood-pressure problems and nervous breakdowns. It makes children irritable, hyperactive and naughty. It is slowly destroying our bodies by 'eating' all the calcium we get from other foods, causing osteoporosis on all seven continents. If these facts shock you, it's a good start. Maybe I will reach some of you and you'll think over your daily abuse of sugar and try to make changes in your diet.

I don't want to induce a fear of any food, not even sugar. It will not harm you if you have a piece of cake with sugar once a month, but if you have a cup of coffee with sugar in it for breakfast, eat a sandwich with white bread for lunch, drink two cups of juice during the day, and cook pasta with canned tomato sauce for dinner, it's likely that you are eating too much of it. And that's without even having a sweet treat!

Having said this, I do use some types of unrefined sugars if other sweeteners will not work as well. This is the case in frostings where finely ground, unrefined Demerara sugar replaces icing/confectioners' sugar to make a fluffy buttercream. It cannot be done with rice or agave syrup. Or, for example, in some cookie recipes, where I want a crunchy texture that cannot be achieved with liquid sweeteners. Also, unrefined sugars taste sweeter than liquid sweeteners, so if I'm making a cocoa cake mixture, I need more sweetness to make up for the bitterness of the cocoa powder.

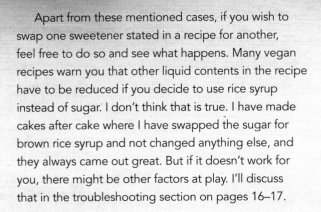

Apart from these mentioned cases, if you wish to swap one sweetener stated in a recipe for another, feel free to do so and see what happens. Many vegan recipes warn you that other liquid contents in the recipe have to be reduced if you decide to use rice syrup instead of sugar. I don't think that is true. I have made cakes after cake where I have swapped the sugar for brown rice syrup and not changed anything else, and they always came out great. But if it doesn't work for you, there might be other factors at play. I'll discuss that in the troubleshooting section on pages 16–17.

Brown rice syrup

I consider brown rice syrup to be the best choice out of all existing sweeteners. Maybe it's because of my background as a macrobiotic chef, but it might also be that it really is the best! Desserts made with it always have a mild taste and are soothing and comforting as opposed to the aggressive taste of conventional sweets. However, there are rice syrups and rice syrups on the market, so to make your shopping easier, here are a few guidelines on how to recognize a good one.

The highest-quality brands of rice syrup (sometimes called rice malt syrup) are traditionally made by a slow, natural enzymatic process out of whole grains. The complex carbohydrates that rice syrup consists of are slowly digested and provide us with stable energy instead of being absorbed immediately and causing rapid surges in blood sugar levels.

Read the labels. If sprouted barley is among the ingredients, the syrup can be used daily. Being thick, somewhat darker and of a slightly distinctive taste, it might not work in every recipe, so have a jar of light brown rice syrup in your kitchen as well. Just be careful to buy organic brands that do not have sugar listed as one of the ingredients!

Barley malt

This is a high-quality sweetener you will find in only one or two recipes in this book, as it has quite a strong taste and is too heavy to be used in desserts you might want to offer to wide audiences. But it's good to have it around and use it in teas, healing hot lemonades, porridges or when making Grissini with Caraway Seeds (see page 120)! It can also be used in pie or cookie doughs, if you don't mind its taste and the dark colour of the resultant baked goodies.

Pure maple syrup

Maple syrup is another good-quality sweetener that, apart from tasting sweet, is rich in trace minerals which act as antioxidants, keep your heart healthy and support your immune system. When shopping for maple syrup, search for pure and organic types that are dark in colour. Make sure there is no added sugar or colouring in the ingredients. I use it in richer cake mixtures and in nut-rich desserts, as well as in many cookie recipes. It gives a deep and rich taste.

Corn and tofu pie
Made with olive oil and soy milk in place of butter and cows' milk

Agave syrup (or nectar)

A highly controversial sweetener, this has been glorified and frowned upon over and over in the past couple of years. Its visual similarity to honey, its strong, sweet taste and its availability in many food stores has made it quite popular and widely used.

It is high in fructose and is quite processed but sometimes you have to make a choice between a bad sweetener (refined sugar) and one that is better, but not ideal at all (in this case, agave syrup). I would put rice and maple syrup highly above it, quality-wise, but if you're in good health, occasional use should not do much harm. Overuse, however, could. Feel free to substitute it with brown rice or maple syrup in each and every one of my recipes. Sometimes its strong, sweet taste is necessary, but if the dessert is slightly less sweet, it's not the end of the world. I don't want to judge agave syrup, but it's important to know the facts and make informed choices. I feel fine using it from time to time but I use the other sweeteners listed much more often.

Unrefined sugars

In cases where there is no substitution possible (as mentioned on page 10), I try to find the best-quality, organic, unrefined sugar that will work well in a specific vegan baking recipe. You might have a better choice, so pick the best one you can. I use Demerara, muscovado and sometimes, if I can get hold of it, sucanat (whole cane sugar). Sugar is sugar, but the unrefined varieties are more wholesome than the highly processed ones, containing minerals and trace elements and taking a little longer to digest.

Oils

Oils play an important role in baking but I use them in smaller amounts than most vegan baking recipes ask for. It's good to think about the dessert you're going to make first and then choose which oil to use, as some oils carry a strong taste that might interfere with other ingredients. Organic, cold-pressed oils are my preferred choice, and even though they are more expensive than highly refined oils, I try to save money on other things and not on the quality of the oil I use daily! There are many other kinds of oil you could use apart from those listed below, depending on what is available to you.

Sunflower oil

Organic, cold-pressed sunflower oil for cooking and baking is an excellent choice that can be used in almost any baking recipe in this book, since it is odourless and mild. It is partially refined to remove the specific taste and smell of sunflower seeds, but being cold pressed makes it healthier than cheap, refined oil. I always have a stash of it in my kitchen as it's excellent for deep frying and sautéing as well.

Extra virgin olive oil

It is not surprising that I try to sneak in olive oil wherever I can; my Mediterranean blood is to blame, and my grandma supplying me with her own Istrian olive oil doesn't help either! I don't mind its slightly bitter taste and I use it in sweet baking a lot, even though this raises a few eyebrows at my baking workshops! Some people say that heat damages good-quality olive oil, and it probably does, but I eat enough of it uncooked, so I'm not afraid to sometimes bake a delicious cake, cookie or cracker with it!

Safflower oil

This oil is made from safflower seeds and is nutritionally similar to sunflower oil. It is high in monounsaturated fats and lower in saturates than olive oil, which makes it quite appealing for healthfood enthusiasts. Another good quality of this oil is its high smoke point, which means it's suitable for high-heat cooking and baking.

Virgin coconut oil

Coconut oil has received much attention and made a big comeback in cooking and baking in the past couple of years. For a long time, it was considered a source of saturated fats which were deemed bad, and this is still

Top to bottom

soy milk, rice milk, coconut milk

true for hydrogenated coconut oil. But today, it is known that some types of saturated fats are good for you and that virgin coconut oil mostly contains healthy fats. It solidifies at lower temperatures so I like to use it instead of margarine in recipes, even though this only works in some cases. It's also delicious!

Non-hydrogenated margarine

I try to avoid using margarine often and in large amounts, and this goes for healthier, non-hydrogenated margarine too. However, some recipes really call for it and we would never have fluffy vegan 'buttercreams' and frostings on cakes and cupcakes were it not for margarine. So, a couple of times a year I make my husband and my guests happy by making layer cakes that resemble conventional cakes so much that no one would ever notice they were made without eggs, refined sugar and dairy!

Non-dairy milks

There is a wide choice of non-dairy milks nowadays, but each type behaves differently in vegan baking recipes. Here are some tips for success in making cakes and cookies that might help you to avoid baking disasters!

Organic, non-gmo, plain soy milk

This is the best liquid for vegan baking as it contains the most protein of all plant milks and is the best alternative to cow's milk in baking, especially in cake mixtures. If it can be replaced by another non-dairy milk, it will be stated in the recipe. Sometimes soy milk may be substituted for soy yogurt. Buy unflavoured, unsweetened milk unless otherwise stated in the recipe.

Coconut milk

This is thick and creamy in texture and has a coconut flavour that works well in some recipes for cake and cookie mixtures. In my opinion, it is more suitable for daily use for people living in a hot climate, but occasional use in baking is a good and tasty change from other non-dairy milks.

Oat milk

This is naturally sweet and works well in frostings and cake creams. It can be combined with soy milk in cake mixtures to give extra moisture but do not add too much as it can cause the cake to break and crumble.

Rice milk

Although lovely and sweet, this is quite watery and contains almost no protein, which is required for good vegan baking. It can be used in some cookies, especially with ground flaxseeds which contribute fat and bulk.

Other plant-based milks

Nut and seed milks can work in some vegan baking recipes but may change the texture, taste or consistency, especially in cakes. I would suggest using them for cake creams and frostings rather than in sensitive cake recipes, particularly if you are not an experienced vegan baker.

Raising agents

Smart use of raising agents is what makes the difference between a heavy cake and a fluffy and light one! I have noticed that many people overuse raising agents in vegan baking to make sure the mixture rises. It's not about quantity but about mixing the best combination to achieve consistent rising results, ie. bicarbonate of/baking soda, baking powder and a little vinegar or lemon juice always results in pure fluffiness!

Aluminium-free baking powder

This has the same rising properties as commercial baking powder, only it's better for you! Also, the flavour of your baked goods will improve substantially as aluminium gives a bitter aftertaste.

Bicarbonate of/baking soda

This is important in vegan baking as it gives that extra 'push' to cake mixtures that might otherwise turn out heavy and dense. It reacts with acidic ingredients and that's why you'll find vinegar, lemon juice, soy yogurt or cocoa alongside it in every recipe of mine.

Active dry yeast (emulsifier-free)

This type of yeast is convenient for long-term storage and must be rehydrated before use. It is sensitive to temperature changes, so avoid exposing the dough to draughts while it is rising.

Thickeners

Of all three thickeners given here, agar is the star and far superior to animal gelatine.

Agar

This natural vegetable gelatine is derived from a red sea vegetable. It is unflavoured, rich in minerals and fibre, and calorie-free. It aids digestion and weight loss, so you could actually be eating a delicious dessert and helping your body to get rid of toxins – pure magic! I cannot understand why conventional dessert-makers do not switch from yucky gelatine (which is made out of pig skin, bovine hides and bones) to this beautiful plant gelatine that feeds you with minerals and makes your desserts delicious, all at the same time! However, it does not make liquids creamy, only firm. That's why, in my cream and frosting recipes, I mostly combine agar with a small amount of cornflour/cornstarch or arrowroot to add creaminess and get a firm texture.

Cornflour/cornstarch

Cornflour/cornstarch is a thickening agent which I use in creams, mousses and frostings, or in cake mixtures to make the cake more elastic and prevent crumbling. It is not the healthiest ingredient, but it is a faithful companion on your road to baking stardom! Try to buy organic, non-gmo cornflour/cornstarch. See also page 8.

Arrowroot powder

This healthy, natural thickener is used in the same way as cornflour/cornstarch but don't use too much of it when thickening creams as it can turn slimy! Heat it only until the mixture thickens, not longer, to prevent thinning. I encourage you to use it but it cannot always replace cornflour/cornstarch so stick to my recipe instructions.

Troubleshooting

Baking is lovely but quite unpredictable, and baking failures can be caused by so many external (and internal) factors, that even if you follow the same cake recipe to the letter, there's no guarantee it will come out the same way it did last time. Especially in vegan baking!

It's good to be aware of this at the beginning of your baking adventures, otherwise you might end up throwing away all your baking cookbooks because you feel no baked goodie ever comes out as the recipe says or as it looks on the photo.

To help you out, here are a couple of things that might happen when you're baking, possible reasons why, and directions as to what to do next time you decide to dirty your bowls, spatulas and baking pans!

Cake

Did not rise? A cake can turn out heavy and dense for many reasons: not sifting dry ingredients, overmixing, using ingredients and pans that are too cold, not preheating the oven, stale baking powder, too much wholemeal/whole-wheat flour compared to unbleached flour, or opening the oven for the first 15 minutes of baking. Maybe the flour used has a very low percentage of protein or you didn't add a crucial acidic ingredient to the batter (lemon, vinegar, etc.).

Sank after baking? Similar reasons to the above. Maybe you threw too many things in at the same time, or your baking pan was too deep and the mixture too liquidy.

Soggy and sticky? It hasn't baked long enough, there was too much liquid in the mixture, or some of the reasons stated in the first two paragraphs. Or you didn't wait for it to cool completely before cutting into it.

Bitter tasting? Too much baking powder that contains aluminium. Use aluminium-free baking powder and measure the amount stated in the recipe carefully.

Cupcake/muffin mixture stuck to the paper cases? You didn't wait long enough for them to cool! Or they are under-baked because your oven is lazy. Buy a good oven thermometer and remember to bake them for longer next time.

Pie and tart crust

Too crumbly to shape? Not enough water. Add a few drops at a time, or just press the dough into the pan without adding any water. Even though it's crumbly, it can result in a good crust because it expands and binds together during baking.

Hard? Definitely overbaked. Maybe you kneaded it too vigorously and for too long, and pie dough hates that. Next time, knead it gently and just enough for the ingredients to come together.

Sticky and oily? It's crucial that the water, flour and margarine are chilled before use, and if they get too warm from the temperature of the kitchen or your warm hands, the oil from the margarine will separate during baking and render an oily and crumbly dough that is impossible to slice.

Soggy bottom? If you are making a pie with a wet filling (like apple pie, etc.) the bottom crust needs to be blind-baked for 7–10 minutes before you fill it. If that isn't done, the bottom crust will not get enough heat and the fruit juice will make it soggy.

Cookies

Dry and hard? They've spent too much time in the oven! Put on a timer next time you bake them because a minute or two too long and they become brown rocks. Maybe there's too much flour in the dough. Did you forget to add the raising agent stated in the recipe?

Floppy instead of crunchy? This always happens if you decide to substitute the unrefined sugar asked for in the recipe with liquid sweetener such as rice syrup or agave. They will still taste great, but they will not be crunchy. Or maybe you stuck to the recipe but you didn't bake them enough, or the temperature was too low? It's important to have a good oven thermometer. *Sticky?* Under-baked. Or did you maybe accidentally add too much liquid?

Pizza and focaccia, before baking

Didn't rise? Some of the reasons could be: the water used to activate the yeast was too cold, or it was too hot and killed the yeast; too much flour used; you didn't knead the dough long enough; the place where the dough was rising was too cool or draughty, or too hot (yeast killed again). Maybe the flour used does not have a high enough percentage of protein, or you left the dough to rise for too long?

Sticky after rising? Too much liquid or not enough flour used, or you didn't knead it long enough.

Yeast dough (and no-knead bread dough), after baking

Pale? Didn't rise long enough before baking. Oven temperature was too low, or the bread is under-baked. Overcrowding the oven might also be a reason for this.

Uneven colour? Your oven is unreliable! Or did you put the bread in the corner, not the middle of the oven?

Heavy, dense and sticky? The yeast was not properly activated or it is stale. The dough was not kneaded long enough, or there was too much flour. Did you forget to take it out of the baking pan after baking and let it cool on a wire rack as stated in the recipe? Did you try to cut into it before it had cooled down completely?

Creams and frostings

Cream didn't set? Not enough agar or uncooked agar. Maybe you didn't leave it to cool in the fridge long enough before slicing. Maybe you substituted soy milk or oat milk for rice milk, which is too watery. Over-cooking arrowroot powder also thins down the cream.

Cream is too hard? Too much agar. It happens often as agar does not thicken the cream while it's hot, so people have a tendency to add more to make sure. Don't do that – trust the recipe. Also, be aware of whether you're using agar powder or flakes, as powder is much stronger and you need to use less of it (1 teaspoon agar powder to 1–2 tablespoons flakes).

Cream is floury? Too much cornflour/cornstarch added, or it was not cooked for long enough.

Cream is lumpy? Either you didn't dilute the thickener at all before adding it to the cream, or you diluted it in warm water and got a lumpy mess. Or you did everything properly, but while pouring it into the hot cream you didn't whisk vigorously enough and the heat was too fierce?

Cream is slimy? Too much arrowroot powder added.

Frosting not fluffy? The margarine was at the wrong temperature – it has to be room temperature, but not too soft and oily. Maybe you didn't sift in the cocoa and sugar, or you added cold liquid into it while creaming.

Chocolate seized/split while melting over a pan of simmering water? Heat is too high, the heatproof bowl is touching the water underneath (don't let it!), you were not stirring continuously or a drop of water found its way into the melting chocolate. Dry the bowl and the whisk/spatula really well and do not cover the chocolate with a lid while it's melting.

Filo/phyllo pastry

Cracked while making strudel? The sheets were left uncovered and dried out. Keep them covered with a damp kitchen towel while you assemble the strudel, and if you have leftover sheets, keep them in the fridge wrapped in clingfilm/plastic wrap or in a sealed bag.

Cracked after baking? Cover the strudel with a dry kitchen towel after baking and allow to cool. This will loosen up the crust. It's a good idea to score the strudel with a sharp knife before baking to mark the place where you want to slice it after baking. This will make your slices neat and the crust will remain undamaged.

basic chocolate cake

Preheat the oven to 180°C (350°F) Gas 4.

Mix together the milk and vinegar in a bowl and set aside for 10 minutes.

Sift the unbleached flour, bicarbonate of/baking soda, baking powder, cocoa and salt into a mixing bowl, then add the wholemeal/whole-wheat flour and cinnamon and mix well.

Add the syrup*, oil and zest to the vinegar mixture and mix well. Gently fold these into the dry ingredients with a spatula. Make sure not to mix too much, otherwise the cake might turn chewy. When everything is just incorporated, spoon the mixture into the prepared cake pan and spread evenly with the spatula.

Bake in the preheated oven for 20–25 minutes or until a skewer inserted in the middle comes out clean. Spring open the cake pan and allow the cake to cool completely.

When the cake is cold, peel off the paper. Slice the cake in half horizontally with a large, serrated knife. You can also cut off the top if it has domed while baking and you prefer it to be flat.

Put the jam and rum or juice in a small saucepan and heat until it comes to the boil. Spread this over both cake layers – this will make the cake moist and stop any frosting from seeping into the cake. Allow to cool.

Put the lower cake layer back in the cake pan and attach the springform ring. The cake is now ready to be topped or filled.

*If you are serving the cake as it is (without a filling or frosting), add a little extra syrup to the mixture, or spread something sweet over the cake after baking.

For a 28-cm/11-in. cake
450 ml/2 cups plain soy milk
1 teaspoon apple cider vinegar
260 g/2 cups unbleached plain/all-purpose flour
1 teaspoon bicarbonate of/baking soda
1 teaspoon baking powder
60 g/⅔ cup cocoa powder
¼ teaspoon salt
60 g/½ cup plain wholemeal/whole-wheat flour
¼ teaspoon ground cinnamon
170 g/⅔ cup pure maple syrup
100 g/½ cup sunflower or safflower oil
grated zest of 1 orange or lemon
125 g/6 tablespoons fruit jam
2 teaspoons rum or juice of ½ orange or lemon

28-cm/11-in. springform cake pan, baselined with parchment paper and oiled

Makes 12–15 slices

For a 23-cm/9-in. cake
300 ml/1⅓ cups plain soy milk
⅔ teaspoon apple cider vinegar
180 g/1⅓ cups unbleached plain/all-purpose flour
⅔ teaspoon bicarbonate of/baking soda
⅔ teaspoon baking powder
40 g/½ cup cocoa powder
a pinch of salt
40 g/⅓ cup plain wholemeal/whole-wheat flour
a pinch of ground cinnamon
120 g/½ cup pure maple syrup
70 g/⅓ cup sunflower or safflower oil
grated zest of 1 orange or lemon
80 g/4 tablespoons fruit jam
2 teaspoons rum or juice of ½ orange or lemon

23-cm/9-in. springform cake pan, baselined with parchment paper and oiled

Makes 8–12 slices

basic nut cake

Preheat the oven to 180°C (350°F) Gas 4.

Mix together the milk and vinegar in a bowl and set aside for 10 minutes.

If you are using whole nuts, grind them finely using a spice mill or food processor.

Sift the unbleached flour, bicarbonate of/baking soda, baking powder, cornflour/cornstarch, vanilla and salt into a mixing bowl, add the nuts, wholemeal/whole-wheat flour and flaxseeds and mix well.

Add the oil and syrup* to the vinegar mixture and mix well. Gently fold these into the dry ingredients with a spatula. Do not mix too much, otherwise the cake might turn chewy. When everything is just incorporated, spoon the mixture into the prepared cake pan and spread evenly with the spatula.

Bake in the preheated oven for 20–25 minutes or until a skewer inserted in the middle comes out clean. Spring open the cake pan and allow the cake to cool completely.

When the cake is cold, peel off the paper. Slice the cake in half horizontally with a large, serrated knife. You can also cut off the top if it has domed while baking and you prefer it to be flat.

Put the jam and rum or juice in a small saucepan and heat until it comes to the boil. Spread this over both cake layers – this will make the cake moist and stop any frosting from seeping into the cake. Allow to cool.

Put the lower cake layer back in the cake pan and attach the springform ring. The cake is now ready to be topped or filled.

*If you are serving the cake as it is (without a filling or frosting), add a little extra syrup to the mixture, or spread something sweet over the cake after baking.

For a 28-cm/11-in. cake
450 ml/2 cups plain soy milk
1 teaspoon apple cider vinegar
60 g/1 cup ground nuts, 60 g/½ cup whole nuts, or 50 g/⅔ cup desiccated coconut
210 g/1⅔ cups unbleached plain/all-purpose flour
1 teaspoon bicarbonate of/baking soda
1½ teaspoons baking powder
40 g/3 tablespoons cornflour/cornstarch
¼ teaspoon bourbon vanilla powder or ½ teaspoon vanilla extract
¼ teaspoon salt
60 g/½ cup plain wholemeal/whole-wheat flour
1 tablespoon ground flaxseeds
100 g/½ cup sunflower or safflower oil
160 g/⅔ cup brown rice syrup
125 g/6 tablespoons fruit jam
2 teaspoons rum or water

28-cm/11-in. springform cake pan, baselined with parchment paper and oiled

Makes 12–15 slices

For a 23-cm/9-in. cake
360 ml/1⅔ cups plain soy milk
⅔ teaspoon apple cider vinegar
50 g/¾ cup ground nuts, 50 g/½ cup whole nuts, or 40 g/⅔ cup desiccated coconut
170 g/1⅓ cups unbleached plain/all-purpose flour
¾ teaspoon bicarbonate of/baking soda
1¼ teaspoons baking powder
30 g/2½ tablespoons cornflour/cornstarch
¼ teaspoon bourbon vanilla powder or ½ teaspoon vanilla extract
a pinch of salt
50 g/⅓ cup plain wholemeal/whole-wheat flour
2½ teaspoons ground flaxseeds
80 g/⅓ cup sunflower or safflower oil
130 g/½ cup brown rice syrup
100 g/5 tablespoons fruit jam
2 teaspoons rum or water

23-cm/9-in. springform cake pan, baselined with parchment paper and oiled

Makes 8–12 slices

sweet pie dough

Put the flour, cornmeal, salt and baking powder in a food processor and pulse to mix. Add the margarine and pulse 6–8 times until the mixture resembles coarse breadcrumbs. Add the syrup and lemon zest and pulse again a couple of times.

Add ice-cold water one tablespoon at a time, pulsing until the mixture just begins to clump together. If you pinch some of the crumbly dough and it holds together, it's ready. If it doesn't, add a little more water and pulse again. Do not add too much water otherwise it will make the dough tough.

Place the dough on a lightly floured work surface. Knead it just enough to form a ball but do not over-knead it. Shape it into a disc, wrap it in clingfilm/plastic wrap and refrigerate it for at least 1 hour, and up to 2 days. If you're in a hurry you can chill the dough in the freezer for 15 minutes. If refrigerated, allow the dough to rest at room temperature for 5–10 minutes before rolling it out.

Preheat the oven to 180°C (350°F) Gas 4 and continue with the relevant recipe.

400 g/3 cups unbleached plain/all-purpose flour
150 g/1 cup fine cornmeal
3 teaspoons baking powder
½ teaspoon salt
240 g/2 cups non-hydrogenated margarine, chilled
130 g/½ cup brown rice or agave syrup
grated zest of 1 lemon
70–110 ml/⅓–½ cup ice-cold water

40 x 28-cm/16 x 11-in. baking pan (for a thinner crust) or 23 x 30 cm/9 x 12-in. baking pan (for a thicker crust)

pizza and focaccia dough

Mix together the starter ingredients in a mixing bowl, cover and allow to rest for 30 minutes.

For the dough, mix together the flours and salt in a bowl. Mix together the water, oil and milk in a jug, then add to the starter and mix well. Finally, add the dry ingredients to the mixing bowl and mix with a wooden spoon.

Place the dough on a lightly floured work surface and knead for 5 minutes or until it is soft and slightly sticky. Add flour as you knead, but not more than necessary. Put the dough in a large, oiled bowl and rub a little oil on the surface of the dough, too. Cover the bowl with a clean, damp towel and allow to rise for 2½ hours in a warm place.

If making pizza, punch the dough down, cover and allow to rise for another 45 minutes.

You can pretend to be a real *pizzaiolo* and stretch the dough with your hands, or use a rolling pin to flatten it to the size of the prepared baking pan. Sprinkle your chosen toppings over it and bake in an oven preheated to 200°C (400°F) Gas 6 for 15–20 minutes.

If making focaccia, shape the dough to fit the prepared baking pan by gently pressing and pushing it from the middle toward the edges. Make dimples by poking the dough with your fingertips. Drizzle with olive oil, cover and allow to rise again for 2 hours.

Sprinkle your chosen seasonings over the dough. Bake in an oven preheated to 180°C (350°F) Gas 4 for 20 minutes, or until golden and crisp.

For the starter
40 g/¼ cup rye flour
55 ml/¼ cup lukewarm water
9 g/2 teaspoons active dry yeast (additive-free)

For the dough
200 g/1½ cups unbleached spelt flour
30 g/¼ cup strong wholemeal/whole-wheat bread flour
½ teaspoon salt
110 ml/½ cup lukewarm water
1 tablespoon olive oil, plus extra for oiling
1 tablespoon soy milk

40 x 28-cm/16 x 11-in. baking pan (for pizza) or 23 x 30 cm/9 x 12-in. baking pan (for focaccia), well oiled

Top and bottom
*pizza and focaccia dough,
sweet pie dough*

CHAPTER 1

Simple cakes & muffins

Breakfast, mid-morning, teatime or for a friend – there are so many occasions suited to simple cakes and muffins. With a gentle emphasis on fresh and dried fruits, nuts and seeds like quinoa, these are recipes to make and eat without guilt or moderation. They will satisfy a sweet craving while giving you a sustained supply of energy.

Muffins CAN be healthy, and full of nutritious ingredients and fibre! Actually, these are perfect for breakfast and are a good substitute for jam on toast when you don't have the time to sit down. Make them the night before, sleep 20 minutes longer in the morning and munch on them on your way to work!

breakfast muffins with apples and jam

Preheat the oven to 180°C (350°F) Gas 4.

Sift together the flours, baking powder, salt and cinnamon in a bowl and mix well.

In a separate bowl, mix together the milk, syrup, oil, lemon juice and zest.

Combine both bowls and mix gently with a silicone spatula. Do not overmix otherwise the muffins will be tough. Add the apples and raisins and gently mix in.

Fill 9 of the muffin cases half-full with the mixture, then put 1 full teaspoon of jam on top. Cover each one with more of the cake mixture, making sure you fill the cases only three-quarters full. If you have any cake mixture left, repeat this process in further muffin cases until you run out of mixture.

Bake in the preheated oven for 30 minutes or until golden.

Remove from the muffin pan and allow to cool on a wire rack.

200 g/1½ cups unbleached plain/all-purpose flour
60 g/½ cup plain wholemeal/whole-wheat flour
2½ teaspoons baking powder
¼ teaspoon salt
½ teaspoon ground cinnamon
300 ml/1¼ cups plain soy milk
130 g/½ cup brown rice syrup
100 g/½ cup safflower or coconut oil
freshly squeezed juice and grated zest of 1 lemon
1 small apple, peeled, cored and diced
60 g/½ cup raisins
100 g/4 tablespoons firm apricot jam (or other)

12-hole muffin pan lined with paper cases

Makes 9–12

Marble cake, marble squares, marble bundt cake – I've been chased by marbled desserts all my life, since every family around me has its own special recipe for this light-dark cake creation. So I made myself a promise that one day I, too, would have my own special marbled dessert recipe! And here it is, in the shape of these wonderfully moist, banana-and-cocoa-flavoured marble muffins. Try to use coconut milk, as I suggest, as it gives a special consistency to the mixture, although using more soy milk instead would also work. The same goes for the cocoa nibs which can be replaced by an additional 1½ tablespoons cocoa powder, but freshly ground nibs will give you an energy kick!

marbled energy muffins

1 tablespoon raw cocoa nibs

130 g/1 cup unbleached plain/
   all-purpose flour

60 g/½ cup plain wholemeal/
   whole-wheat flour

¼ teaspoon bourbon vanilla
   powder

1 teaspoon baking powder

½ teaspoon bicarbonate of/
   baking soda

¼ teaspoon salt

100 g/½ cup coconut oil

110 ml/½ cup coconut milk

170 ml/¾ cup plain soy milk

½ teaspoon apple cider
   vinegar

170 g/⅔ cup pure maple
   syrup

1 ripe banana

¼ teaspoon pure almond
   extract (optional)

grated zest of 1 lemon

1 tablespoon raw cocoa
   powder

*12-hole muffin pan lined
   with paper cases*

Makes 10–12

Preheat the oven to 180°C (350°F) Gas 4.

In a coffee or spice grinder, grind the cocoa nibs to a coarse powder.

Sift together the flours, vanilla powder, baking powder, bicarbonate of/baking soda and salt in a bowl and mix well.

If the coconut oil has solidified, put the jar in a bowl of hot water until the oil has softened. Put the coconut oil, milks, vinegar, syrup, banana, almond extract, if using, and lemon zest in a food processor and blend until smooth.

Combine the dry and liquid ingredients, and mix gently with a silicone spatula.

Spoon one third of the mixture into a separate bowl and fold in the ground cocoa nibs and cocoa powder.

Divide the plain cake mixture between 10–12 muffin cases. Put a spoonful of the cocoa mixture on top of that and, with the help of a chopstick or skewer, mix a little to get a marbled pattern.

Bake in the preheated oven for 18–20 minutes.

Remove from the muffin pan and allow to cool on a wire rack. This is a great picnic and lunchbox muffin!

This is a very simple recipe for muffins that are juicy, fruity and a little nutty too! Adding toasted wheat germ gives them a nice golden colour as well as providing a little extra taste, minerals, vitamins and fibre. Find it in your local healthfood store and use it not only in baking but also in cereals, salads and smoothies.

summer muffins with raspberries and blackberries

Preheat the oven to 180°C (350°F) Gas 4.

Sift together the flours, bicarbonate of/baking soda, baking powder and salt in a bowl and add the ground hazelnuts and wheat germ, if using. Mix well.

Put the milk, syrup, oil, lemon juice and apple in a food processor and blend until smooth.

Combine the dry and liquid ingredients, and mix gently with a silicone spatula. Do not overmix otherwise the muffins will be tough.

Divide the cake mixture between the muffin cases. Gently press 2 raspberries and 2 blackberries into each muffin so that they are half-dipped in the mixture.

Bake in the preheated oven for 25–30 minutes.

Allow to cool in the muffin pan for a few minutes, then transfer to a wire rack to cool completely.

Enjoy the muffins on the beach, by the pool, on a picnic in the shade or wherever you like to spend sunny summer days!

325 g/2½ cups unbleached plain-all-purpose flour
65 g/½ cup plain wholemeal/whole-wheat flour
1½ teaspoons bicarbonate of/baking soda
1 teaspoon baking powder
¼ teaspoon salt
65 g/1 cup finely ground hazelnuts
25 g/3 tablespoons toasted wheat germ (optional)
420 ml/1¾ cups plain soy milk
200 g/¾ cup brown rice syrup
150 g/¾ cup sunflower oil
freshly squeezed juice of ½ lemon
100 g/1 small apple, peeled, cored and chopped
24 raspberries
24 blackberries

12-hole muffin pan lined with paper cases

Makes 12

It is an old tradition in Istria, Croatia, for wedding guests to bring a light pound cake (originally Italian) called 'pan di Spagna'. Each guest adds a unique touch to their cake with their choice of nuts, fruits and decoration. This is my vegan version of 'pan di Spagna', or if you like, 'pan d'Istria'!

pan di spagna

90 g/⅔ cup fine cornmeal

120 g/1 cup unbleached plain/ all-purpose flour

45 g/⅓ cup plain wholemeal/ whole-wheat flour

3 teaspoons baking powder

1 teaspoon bicarbonate of/ baking soda

¼ teaspoon salt

¼ teaspoon bourbon vanilla powder

60 g/½ cup pine nuts

40 g/¼ cup chopped walnuts

150 ml/⅔ cup plain soy milk

1 teaspoon apple cider vinegar

65 g/⅓ cup olive oil

85 g/⅓ cup brown rice or agave syrup

2 tablespoons Grappa (grape-based brandy), brandy or rum

grated zest and freshly squeezed juice of 1 lemon

90 g/⅔ cup chopped dried figs

finely ground unrefined sugar, for dusting

23-cm/9-in. springform cake pan, baselined with parchment paper and oiled

Serves about 10

Preheat the oven to 180°C (350°F) Gas 4.

Sift together the cornmeal, flours, baking powder, bicarbonate of/baking soda, salt and vanilla powder in a bowl and mix well. Add the pine nuts and walnuts and mix.

In a separate bowl, mix together the milk, vinegar, oil, syrup, alcohol, lemon juice and zest. Add the figs and incorporate well.

Combine both bowls and mix gently with a silicone spatula until well combined. Do not overmix otherwise the cake will be chewy and won't rise well.

Spoon the cake mixture into the prepared cake pan and spread level with the spatula. Bake in the preheated oven for 30–35 minutes.

Allow the cake to cool completely before removing it from the pan. If you wish, dust the top of the cold cake with a little finely ground unrefined sugar just before serving.

Castagnaccio, or chestnut cake, is a traditional Tuscan dessert and one of the few Italian desserts that doesn't require a lot of sugar and eggs! Since the Istrian peninsula is also rich in chestnut trees, I grew up eating many different chestnut-based dishes, both sweet and savoury. This cake is something in between; the chestnut flour gives it a mild sweet taste but since no other sweetener is used, it's not the typically sweet cake you might expect. However, it's still wonderfully simple and tasty – once a poor man's dessert, it's now a delicacy enjoyed by gourmets around the world! And totally vegan!

castagnaccio

Soak the raisins in a bowl of the rum and 2 tablespoons hot water while you prepare the other ingredients.

Preheat the oven to 200°C (400°F) Gas 6.

Sift together the flour, salt, vanilla powder in a bowl, then mix in the orange zest and half of the oil. Slowly whisk in the milk, adding just enough to get a smooth, soft batter; it should be soft enough to fall from the whisk, but not too liquid.

Drain the soaked raisins and pat them dry, then add them to the cake mixture.

Pour the mixture into the prepared cake pan until about 2 cm/¾ inch thick in the pan – shallower is fine but deeper could result in a soggy texture.

Sprinkle the pine nuts, hazelnuts and rosemary needles evenly over the top of the cake and press them in lightly. Drizzle some of the remaining olive oil over the top.

Bake in the preheated oven for 30–40 minutes, or until a thin, cracked crust has formed. The inside should still be soft and moist. Allow to cool completely in the pan.

Serve the cake with a dollop of whipped soy cream or a drizzle of agave syrup. It will keep for a couple of days in an airtight container.

60 g/½ cup raisins
1 tablespoon rum
300 g/2⅓ cups chestnut flour
¼ teaspoon salt
¼ teaspoon bourbon vanilla powder
grated zest of 1 orange
50 g/¼ cup olive oil
450–625 ml/2–3 cups rice milk
60 g/⅓ cup pine nuts
60 g/⅓ cup chopped hazelnuts
needles pulled from 1 fresh rosemary sprig
whipped soy cream or agave syrup, to serve

24-cm/9½-in. springform cake pan, well oiled

Serves about 8

I love the taste and texture of this cake and the addition of sweet potato adds extra vitamin A and fibre while making it visually interesting. I also like using pumpkin or rhubarb in the same way, when sweet potatoes aren't available.

sweet-potato pound cake

125 g/1 full cup peeled and cubed sweet potato

130 g/1 cup unbleached plain/all-purpose flour

65 g/½ cup plain wholemeal/whole-wheat flour

1 teaspoon bicarbonate of/baking soda

1 teaspoon baking powder

¼ teaspoon salt

100 g/½ cup raw/unrefined brown sugar

110 ml/½ cup sparkling mineral water

3 tablespoons apple concentrate (see method for an alternative)

65 g/⅓ cup sunflower oil

100 g/⅔ cup plain, soft tofu

100 ml/½ cup oat or soy cream

1-kg/2-lb. loaf pan, neatly lined with parchment paper (if you snip diagonally into the corners of the paper, it will fit more snuggly into the pan)

Makes 8–10 slices

Preheat the oven to 180°C (350°F) Gas 4.

Steam the cubes of sweet potato for 10 minutes or until they are soft, but they should not fall apart when you prick them.

Sift together the flours, bicarbonate of/baking soda, baking powder and salt in a bowl and mix well.

Mix together the sparkling water and apple concentrate. You can use apple juice instead, but the sparkling water works well with bicarbonate of/baking soda and baking powder and makes this cake moist and spongy.

In a separate bowl, mix together the apple juice, oil, tofu and cream until smooth.

Combine the dry and liquid ingredients and mix until smooth. Fold in the steamed cubes of potato, reserving a couple of pieces for decoration.

Pour the mixture into the prepared loaf pan and spread level with a spatula. Sprinkle the reserved potatoes over the top and press them in lightly.

Bake the cake in the preheated oven for 25 minutes or until a skewer inserted in the middle comes out clean. Allow to cool in the pan for 10 minutes, then remove it, peel off the paper and allow to cool completely on a wire rack.

Serve a slice of the cake with a cup of warm green tea scented with lemon or lime. The best way to keep the cake moist is wrapped in a clean kitchen towel.

This is a recipe for (in my opinion) a healthy combination of ingredients which are transformed, with a little love and effort, into a very tasty loaf that will make the whole family happy. Not to mention the fact that many ingredients in this recipe can be replaced with any of the fruits, seeds and nuts that have been cluttering your kitchen cupboards for months!

rich tea bread

Chop all the dried fruit into pieces roughly the same size as the raisins. Take the strong, hot tea and pour over the chopped fruit in a mixing bowl. Allow it to steep for at least 30 minutes or longer.

Preheat the oven to 180°C (350°F) Gas 4.

Add the syrup, orange juice and zest and the oil to the bowl of soaked fruit and mix well.

In a separate bowl, mix together the flour, baking powder, bicarbonate of/baking soda, salt, cinnamon, nutmeg, ginger, cashews, walnuts and hazelnuts or pine nuts. Add them to the fruit mixture and mix again with a wooden spoon until incorporated.

Spoon the cake mixture into the prepared loaf pan and spread level with a spatula. Bake in the preheated oven for 45–55 minutes or until a skewer inserted in the middle comes out clean. Allow to cool in the pan for 10 minutes, then remove and allow to cool completely on a wire rack.

Serve a slice of the cake with a cup of hot tea, of the same type used in the cake!

60 g/½ cup dried plums
60 g/½ cup dates
40 g/⅓ cup dried cranberries
2 tablespoons dried goji berries
60 g/½ cup raisins
330 ml/1½ cups strong, hot tea (eg. rosehip and aniseed)
3 tablespoons brown rice or pure maple syrup
freshly squeezed juice and grated zest of 1 orange
65 g/⅓ cup sunflower oil
200 g/1½ cups flour (eg. unbleached spelt flour plus unbleached plain/all-purpose flour)
1 teaspoon baking powder
1 teaspoon bicarbonate of/baking soda
¼ teaspoon salt
½ teaspoon ground cinnamon
¼ teaspoon ground nutmeg
¼ teaspoon ground ginger
110 g/⅔ cup chopped cashews
110 g/⅔ cup chopped walnuts
3 tablespoons chopped hazelnuts or pine nuts

1-kg/2-lb. loaf pan, oiled

Makes 8–10 slices

These are not just any scones; they are full of fibre and nutrients and totally sugar-free! Quinoa must be the most often used grain in my kitchen so I always have some leftovers in the fridge. One day I came up with a great way to use some of that by adding pre-cooked quinoa to my scone dough! A touch of dried fruit and agave syrup gives them a mild sweet taste, so you should top them with your favourite fruit jam if you're craving a sweet treat. These scones are a great breakfast, a great snack, great as travel food; actually they are great any time of the day, wherever you are!

quinoa scones

5 tablespoons cooked quinoa (see method for an alternative)
130 g/1 cup unbleached plain/all-purpose flour
60 g/½ cup plain wholemeal/whole-wheat flour
2 teaspoons baking powder
½ teaspoon salt
45 g/¼ cup non-hydrogenated margarine, chilled
1 tablespoon coarse cornmeal/polenta
110 ml/½ cup buttermilk (made from 110 ml/½ cup soy milk mixed with ½ teaspoon apple cider vinegar and left to rest for 5–10 minutes)
30 g/¼ cup dried fruit of your choice (raisins, dates, etc.)
3 tablespoons brown rice or agave syrup

baking sheet lined with parchment paper

Makes 10

If you want to cook the quinoa from scratch, boil 250 ml/1 cup water in a saucepan, then add 90 g/½ cup quinoa and a pinch of salt. Lower the heat and simmer for 20 minutes or until the quinoa has absorbed all the water. Allow the quinoa to cool.

Preheat the oven to 200°C (400°F) Gas 6.

Sift together the flours, baking powder and salt in a bowl. Add the margarine and rub it into the dry ingredients until the mixture resembles fine breadcrumbs. Stir in the quinoa and coarse cornmeal/polenta.

In a separate bowl, mix the buttermilk, dried fruit and syrup. Pour it into the dry ingredients and mix briefly with a spatula until you get a soft dough.

Divide the dough into 10 spoonfuls and drop onto the prepared baking sheet, leaving a little space between them. Pat down the tops to neaten them.

Bake in the preheated oven for 15–20 minutes or until risen and golden. Allow to cool slightly on the baking sheet.

The scones are great served warm, fresh from the oven with a dollop of jam, but they are also yummy eaten cold, reheated in the oven, or toasted just before serving.

CHAPTER 2

Fancy cakes

For a birthday, special dinner, vegan tea party, Mother's Day, Father's Day and everything in between – this is your chance to pull out all the stops. These fancy cakes are layered, rich, show-stopping, and made with love. So set aside a bit of time, put your apron on, turn the radio up and enjoy baking a special cake for a special someone.

This is THE most popular cake of all the ones I make for both children's and grown-ups' birthdays! It's full of chocolate flavour, moist and very light. Don't tell your guests it's vegan and sugar-free, wait for their reaction, then confess! Nobody can ever tell this cake is super-healthy.

chocolate layer cake

For the Basic Chocolate Cake on page 18, decide which size you want to make before you start: a 28-cm/11-in. cake for 8–12 slices or a 23-cm/9-in. cake for 12–15 slices, then follow the corresponding instructions. When you've baked the cake and prepared it as described on page 18, put the bottom layer back in the cake pan and set the top layer aside while you make the filling.

For the chocolate cream, put the milk and syrup in a large saucepan and add the cocoa powder and agar. Whisk and bring to the boil over medium heat. As soon as it comes to the boil, lower the heat before it bubbles over and makes a mess! Now boil gently for 4–5 minutes if you are using agar powder, or 10–12 minutes if you are using flakes or until the flakes have completely melted.

Mix the cornflour/cornstarch into 3 tablespoons cold water.

Add the chocolate to the hot cream, whisking vigorously until completely melted, then lower the heat to its lowest and slowly add the cornflour/cornstarch mixture, still whisking vigorously. Bring to the boil, then remove from the heat. Allow to cool and thicken slightly – about 20 minutes. Whisk just to mix, then divide in half.

Ladle one portion of the warm cream on top of the cake layer in its sealed cake pan. Allow to set for 10 minutes or until a thin film forms on the top, then carefully cover with the second cake layer. Wait for a couple of minutes, then slowly ladle the second portion of cream on top. Allow to cool to room temperature, then refrigerate for at least 6 hours or overnight.

When you are ready to serve, slide a spatula between the cake and the pan to loosen it. Release the pan. The cake should be nice and firm, with a shiny cream all around it. Decorate with chocolate shavings and cut into slices with a sharp knife dipped in hot water.

The cake keeps in the fridge in an airtight container for 5 days.

Basic Chocolate Cake (page 18, but see method here)
vegan chocolate shavings, to decorate

For the chocolate cream
1.5 litres/6 cups chocolate soy or oat milk
195 g/¾ cup agave syrup
2 tablespoons cocoa powder
2½ teaspoons agar powder or 7 teaspoons agar flakes
3 tablespoons cornflour/ cornstarch
100 g/scant ¾ cup finely chopped vegan dark/ bittersweet chocolate (70% cocoa)

28-cm/11-in. or 23-cm/9-in. springform cake pan, baselined with parchment paper and oiled (see method)

Serves 12–15

If you're nuts about nuts, especially hazelnuts, you'll be in heaven after a slice of this cake! Nuts were often used for baking in both my grandmas' kitchens and I favour them too, particularly in the autumn and winter.

hazelnut heaven cake

Basic Nut Cake (page 19, using hazelnuts and referring to method here)
120 g/¾ cup toasted hazelnuts, roughly chopped, to decorate

For the hazelnut cream
1.5 litres/6 cups vanilla soy or oat milk
195 g/¾ cup brown rice syrup
2½ teaspoons agar powder or 7 teaspoons agar flakes
160 g/1 cup toasted hazelnuts or 100 g/½ cup hazelnut butter
3 tablespoons vanilla pudding powder or cornflour/ cornstarch

28-cm/11-in. or 23-cm/9-in. springform cake pan, baselined with parchment paper and oiled (see method)

Serves 12–15

For the Basic Nut Cake on page 19, decide which size you want to make before you start: a 28-cm/11-in. cake for 8–12 slices or a 23-cm/9-in. cake for 12–15 slices, then follow the corresponding instructions, using hazelnuts. When you've baked the cake and prepared it as described on page 19, put the bottom layer back in the cake pan and set the top layer aside while you make the filling.

For the hazelnut cream, put the milk and syrup in a large saucepan and add the agar. Whisk and bring to the boil over medium heat. As soon as it comes to the boil, lower the heat before it bubbles over and makes a mess! Now boil gently for 4–5 minutes if you are using agar powder, or 10–12 minutes if you are using flakes or until the flakes have completely melted.

Meanwhile, if using whole toasted hazelnuts, grind 100 g/⅔ cup of the 160 g/1 cup and finely grind them in a spice mill or food processor. Coarsely chop the rest and set aside.

Mix the vanilla powder or cornflour/cornstarch into 3 tablespoons cold water.

Add the ground nuts or nut butter to the hot cream, whisking vigorously until completely incorporated, then lower the heat to its lowest and slowly add the vanilla powder or cornflour/cornstarch mixture, still whisking vigorously. Bring to the boil, then remove from the heat. Allow to cool and thicken slightly – about 20 minutes. Whisk just to mix, then divide in half.

Ladle one portion of the warm cream on top of the cake layer in its sealed cake pan. Sprinkle the reserved chopped hazelnuts all over the cream. Allow to set for 10 minutes or until a thin film forms on the top, then carefully cover with the second cake layer. Wait for a couple of minutes, then slowly ladle the second portion of cream on top. Allow to cool to room temperature, then refrigerate for at least 6 hours or overnight.

When you are ready to serve, slide a spatula between the cake and the pan to loosen it. Release the pan. The cake should be nice and firm, with a shiny cream all around it. To decorate, scatter the chopped 120 g/¾ cup hazelnuts over the cake and cut into slices with a sharp knife dipped in hot water.

The cake keeps in the fridge in an airtight container for 5 days.

This cake is my husband's firm favourite! If you also like cakes that are more robust and quite filling, this should be your choice. It's a great recipe as it's quite simple and you can use other fruit instead of strawberries; I often use sour cherries, but bananas are great too, especially if the cake is for guests with a serious sweet tooth!

double cocoa and strawberry cake

For the Basic Chocolate Cake on page 18, decide which size you want to make before you start: a 28-cm/11-in. cake for 8–12 slices or a 23-cm/9-in. cake for 12–15 slices, then follow the corresponding instructions. When you've baked the cake and prepared it as described on page 18, put the bottom layer on a serving plate and set the top layer aside while you make the filling.

For the cocoa buttercream, very finely grind the brown sugar in a spice mill or food processor; you should get about 2 cups powdered sugar.

Sift together the cocoa powder and powdered brown sugar in a bowl. Stir in the vanilla powder.

In a separate, large bowl, beat the margarine with an electric whisk until soft. Gradually add the sifted ingredients, beating well and adding a little milk when the mixture gets dry. Continue to beat until the buttercream is light and fluffy – this will take a couple of minutes, so be patient!

Hull and slice half of the strawberries. Hull and halve the remaining strawberries (or leave some unhulled if you prefer – these will be used to decorate the top of the cake).

Spread half of the cocoa buttercream over the bottom cake layer with a spatula. Arrange the strawberry slices over the buttercream, then cover with the top cake layer. Spread the remaining buttercream over the top of the cake.

Decorate with the strawberry halves.

Store the cake in the fridge, but bring to room temperature for 30 minutes before serving, as the buttercream firms up when chilled.

Basic Chocolate Cake (page 18, but see method here)
500 g/1 lb. strawberries

For the cocoa buttercream
200 g/1 cup Demerara or other good-quality brown sugar (or icing/confectioners' sugar – see method)
150 g/1⅔ cups cocoa powder
½ teaspoon bourbon vanilla powder
450 g/3¼ cups non-hydrogenated margarine, at room temperature
2–3 tablespoons plain soy milk, at room temperature

28-cm/11-in. or 23-cm/9-in. springform cake pan, baselined with parchment paper and oiled (see method)

Serves 12–15

I love finding kumquats at farmers' markets; their sweet citrus smell always inspires me to find new ways to use them in recipes. Here I've created a cake in which kumquats and lemons balance the heavier cocoa and buttercream. I love the contrast of dark cake with white frosting and bright orange kumquat circles. If you've never tried these lovely little citrus fruits, you must! They are eaten whole (peel and all) and the peel is ultra sweet while the interior is sharp and juicy. If you can't find them, you can decorate the cake with thin segments of orange instead.

black and white cake with lemon buttercream

Basic Chocolate Cake (page 18, but see method here)
about 8 kumquats, washed, to decorate

For the lemon buttercream
200 g/1 cup Demerara sugar or other good-quality brown sugar (or icing/confectioners' sugar – see method)
500 g/3½ cups non-hydrogenated margarine, at room temperature
7 tablespoons freshly squeezed lemon juice
2–3 tablespoons finely grated lemon zest
¼ teaspoon bourbon vanilla powder
2 tablespoons plain soy milk, at room temperature

23-cm/9-in. springform cake pan, baselined with parchment paper and oiled

Serves about 12

Make and bake the Basic Chocolate Cake on page 18, then when it has cooled and you have prepared it as described on page 18, put the bottom layer on a serving plate and set the top layer aside while you make the filling.

For the lemon buttercream, very finely grind the brown sugar in a spice mill or food processor; you should get about 2 cups powdered sugar.

In a separate, large bowl, beat the margarine with an electric whisk until soft. Gradually add the powdered brown sugar half a cup at a time, together with a splash of lemon juice. Beat well and keep adding sugar and lemon juice until you have used them all up. Add the lemon zest and the vanilla powder, and a little of the milk, if it is too dry. Mix again until light and fluffy.

Spread one-third of the lemon buttercream over the bottom cake layer with a spatula. Cover with the top cake layer and spread the remaining buttercream over the top and side of the cake, covering it as evenly and neatly as you can.

To decorate, thinly slice the kumquats (peel included) and arrange over the top of the cake.

Store the cake in the fridge, but bring to room temperature for 30 minutes before serving, as the buttercream firms up when chilled! Enjoy!

Schwarzwald, or Black-Forest cake is so very popular with my friends and family that I had to come up with a vegan version of it, and when I finally did, I made it into these cupcakes! The chocolate-cherry-whipped-cream combination is a winner, and the high quality of the ingredients used makes them so much tastier than other Schwarzwald desserts!

black-forest-gâteau cupcakes

Preheat the oven to 180°C (350°F) Gas 4.

Mix together the flours, semolina/farina, cocoa powder, baking powder, bicarbonate of/baking soda and salt in a bowl.

In a separate bowl, mix together the oil, syrup, milk, lemon juice and zest. Pour into the bowl of dry ingredients and mix gently with a wooden spoon until just incorporated. Fold in the chocolate.

Divide the cake mixture between the muffin cases.

Bake in the preheated oven for 20–25 minutes. Allow to cool for a few minutes, then remove the cupcakes from the muffin pan and allow to cool completely on a wire rack.

For the chocolate frosting, melt the chocolate in a heatproof bowl set over a saucepan of simmering water. Do not let the base of the bowl touch the water. Meanwhile, heat the milk in a pan until just before boiling. Pour the melted chocolate into the hot milk and whisk until smooth. Add the syrup and mix well. Allow to cool for 45 minutes or until set.

Drain the cherries, saving the Kirsch. Mix the arrowroot into a couple of teaspoons of cold water, then stir into the reserved Kirsch in a pan. Set over medium heat and whisk until it thickens a little – about 2 minutes.

Scoop a little well out of the top of each cooled cupcake with a teaspoon. Carefully pour about 1 teaspoon Kirsch syrup in each well. Place a cherry in there too. Briefly whisk the cooled chocolate frosting, then spread over the cupcakes. Spoon a dollop of whipped soy cream onto each cupcake, top with a couple of cherries and a drizzle of the Kirsch syrup. Serve immediately!

130 g/1 cup unbleached plain/
   all-purpose flour
65 g/½ cup plain wholemeal/
   whole-wheat flour
80 g/½ cup semolina/farina
45 g/½ cup cocoa powder
2 teaspoons baking powder
1 teaspoon bicarbonate of/
   baking soda
¼ teaspoon salt
100 g/½ cup sunflower oil
260 g/1 cup brown rice syrup
170 ml/¾ cup plain soy milk
1 teaspoon freshly squeezed
   lemon juice
grated zest of 2 lemons
60 g/½ cup chopped vegan
   dark/bittersweet chocolate
360 g/1½ cups cherries in
   Kirsch
1 teaspoon arrowroot powder
whipped soy cream,
   to decorate

For the chocolate frosting
130 g/1 cup finely chopped
   vegan dark/bittersweet
   chocolate
50 ml/scant ¼ cup non-dairy milk
2 tablespoons brown rice syrup

*12-hole muffin pan lined with
   paper cupcake cases*

Makes 12

My friend Sanja wanted to surprise her boyfriend with a cake that combined two of his favourite flavours: pineapple and coconut. After serious thinking, testing and retesting, I came up with this, the ultimate summer cake.

exotic pineapple and coconut cake

Basic Nut Cake (page 19, using
   desiccated coconut and referring
   to method here)

For the coconut cream
500 ml/2¼ cups plain or vanilla
   soy or oat milk
150 g/generous ½ cup brown
   rice syrup
1 teaspoon agar powder or
   2 teaspoons agar flakes
1 small apple
55 g/3 tablespoons non-
   hydrogenated margarine
330 g/1½ cups vanilla soy custard
140 g/1¾ cups desiccated coconut,
   plus extra, toasted, to decorate
3 tablespoons cornflour/cornstarch

For the pineapple cream
1 litre/4⅓ cups vanilla soy
   or oat milk
100 g/generous ⅓ cup brown
   rice syrup
1½ teaspoons agar powder
   or 5 teaspoons agar flakes
300 g/2 cups cubed fresh or
   canned pineapple
230 ml/1 cup soy cream
grated zest of 1 lemon
2 tablespoons cornflour/cornstarch

*28-cm/11-in. or 23-cm/9-in.
   springform cake pan, baselined
   with parchment paper and oiled
   (see method)*

Serves 12–15

For the coconut cream, put the milk and 85 g/⅓ cup of the syrup in a large saucepan and add the agar. Whisk and bring to the boil, then lower the heat and simmer for 3 minutes if you are using agar powder, or 8 minutes if using flakes or until the flakes have completely melted.

Peel, core and chop the apple, then put in a food processor with the margarine, remaining syrup and custard. Blend until smooth, then fold in the coconut. Mix the cornflour/cornstarch into 3 tablespoons cold water.

Add the coconut mixture to the hot milk, whisking vigorously until incorporated, then lower the heat to its lowest and slowly add the cornflour/cornstarch mixture, still whisking vigorously. Bring to the boil, then remove from the heat. Pour it on top of the cake layer in its sealed cake pan and spread level with a spatula, then carefully cover with the second cake layer and press gently.

For the pineapple cream, put the milk and syrup in a large saucepan, add the agar and cook as above.

Put the pineapple, cream and lemon zest in a food processor and blend until smooth. Mix the cornflour/cornstarch into 2 tablespoons cold water.

Add the pineapple mixture to the hot milk, whisking vigorously until incorporated, then lower the heat to its lowest and slowly add the cornflour/cornstarch mixture, still whisking vigorously. Bring to the boil, then remove from the heat. Ladle two-thirds of the cream on top of the second cake layer in the pan. Refrigerate the remaining cream for later. Allow the cake to cool to room temperature, then refrigerate for at least 6 hours or overnight.

When you are ready to serve, slide a spatula between the cake and the pan to loosen it. Release the pan. The cake should be nice and firm, with a shiny cream all around it. Briefly whisk the refrigerated pineapple cream until smooth, then spread around the side of the cake with a spatula.

Scatter toasted desiccated coconut over the top and cut into slices with a sharp knife dipped in hot water.

The cake keeps in the fridge in an airtight container for 5 days.

According to a survey from 2011, carrot cake was voted as the favourite cake in the UK! I'm offering you a recipe that contains the expected ingredients (carrots, walnuts, raisins) but it is sweetened with maple syrup, it's low in fat and the frosting is very light.

rich carrot cake

Preheat the oven to 180°C (350°F) Gas 4.

Sift together the flours, baking powder, bicarbonate of/ baking soda, salt and cinnamon in a bowl, add the desiccated coconut and vanilla powder and mix well.

If the coconut oil has solidified, put the jar in a bowl of hot water until the oil has softened.

In a separate bowl, mix together the syrup, coconut oil, orange juice and zest, vinegar and rum.

Combine both bowls and mix until smooth. Add the carrots, raisins and walnuts and fold in with a spatula. The mixture will be thicker than a normal cake mixture.

Spoon the cake mixture into the prepared cake pan and spread level with a spatula. Bake in the preheated oven for 30 minutes. Allow to cool completely in the pan.

For the frosting, put all the ingredients in a small saucepan and whisk well for the cornflour/cornstarch to dissolve. Set over medium heat and whisk vigorously for a couple of minutes. As the milk starts to warm up, the cornflour/cornstarch will start to thicken it. As soon as the frosting is thick enough to spread, remove it from heat.

Remove the cake from the pan and spread the hot frosting over the top with a spatula. Allow to cool completely.

Decorate the cake with orange zest and drizzle a little maple syrup on each slice to make it sweeter, if you like.

200 g/1½ cups unbleached plain/ all-purpose flour
65 g/½ cup plain wholemeal/ whole-wheat flour
1 teaspoon baking powder
1 teaspoon bicarbonate of/ baking soda
¼ teaspoon salt
1 teaspoon ground cinnamon
40 g/1 cup desiccated coconut
½ teaspoon bourbon vanilla powder
100 g/½ cup coconut oil
170 g/⅔ cup pure maple syrup
freshly squeezed juice and grated zest of 1 orange, plus extra to decorate
½ teaspoon apple cider vinegar
1 teaspoon rum
330 g/3 cups grated carrots
60 g/½ cup raisins
80 g/½ cup chopped walnuts

For the frosting
220 ml/1 cup oat milk
2 tablespoons oat or soy cream
3 tablespoons pure maple syrup
3 scant tablespoons cornflour/ cornstarch
½ teaspoon bourbon vanilla powder
6 drops of pure orange extract or 1 tablespoon finely grated orange zest

23-cm/9-in. springform cake pan, baselined with parchment paper and oiled

Serves about 8

CHAPTER 3

Slices & bars

For lunchboxes, picnics and after-school treats – these slices and bars are usually nutritious, often portable and always delicious! Some of the recipes in this chapter are so simple that children can help you make them. They will love to get their hands messy and then to tuck into the fruits of their labours afterwards.

Carob is native to the Mediterranean region but can now be found in stores everywhere – as powder, syrup, drops, spread, etc. It is sometimes used as a cocoa substitute as it tastes similar but contains no caffeine. These slices are sweet and full of carob flavour, and most people who have never tasted carob before say that it was love at first bite!

yummy carob slices

Preheat the oven to 180°C (350°F) Gas 4.

Heat 250 ml/1 cup of the milk in a large saucepan until hot but not boiling, then remove from the heat, add the carob 'chocolate' and allow to melt.

Mix together the remaining milk and the vinegar in a bowl and set aside for 2–3 minutes.

Stir the melted carob until smooth, then add the vinegar mixture. Add the syrup, oil and flaxseeds and whisk until combined.

Sift together the flours, carob powder, bicarbonate of/baking soda, baking powder, salt and vanilla powder in a mixing bowl.

Slowly pour the wet ingredients into the sifted dry ingredients, mixing with a wooden spoon. Do not overmix but try to get a smooth mixture without too many lumps.

Spoon the cake mixture into the prepared baking pan and spread level with a spatula. Bake in the preheated oven for 30 minutes or until a skewer inserted in the middle comes out clean. Allow to cool completely in the pan.

For the carob glaze, mix the cornflour/cornstarch into 4 tablespoons cold water.

Put the milk, syrup, carob powder and agar in a saucepan and mix well. Bring to the boil, then lower the heat and simmer for a couple of minutes. Slowly add the cornflour/cornstarch mixture, whisking vigorously. Bring to the boil, then remove from the heat.

Pour the hot carob glaze over the cooled cake in the pan. Spread it with a spatula and allow to cool at room temperature for 1–2 hours.

Dust with carob powder and cut into slices to serve.

675 ml/3 cups plain soy milk
100 g/3½ oz. carob 'chocolate', finely chopped
2 teaspoons apple cider vinegar
195 g/¾ cup brown rice syrup
150 g/¾ cup sunflower oil
1 tablespoon ground flaxseeds
415 g/3 cups plus 2 tablespoons unbleached plain/all-purpose flour
65 g/½ cup plain wholemeal/ whole-wheat flour
75 g/¾ cup carob powder, for dusting
1½ teaspoons bicarbonate of/ baking soda
1½ teaspoons baking powder
½ teaspoon salt
¼ teaspoon bourbon vanilla powder

For the carob glaze
3 tablespoons cornflour/ cornstarch
550 ml/2 cups non-dairy milk
170 g/⅔ cup carob syrup or pure maple syrup
180 g/1¾ cups carob powder
1 teaspoon agar powder or 2 teaspoons agar flakes

40 x 28-cm/16 x 11-in. baking pan, lined with parchment paper

Makes about 20

I remember eating a dessert similar to this one at my neighbour's house a couple of times and I really liked the texture, but the taste of butter in the glaze was too strong and the cake was too sweet. So I made a vegan version of it, leaving semolina/farina as the main ingredient but adapting it to my taste. You can also use half semolina/farina and half unbleached flour, but the grainy texture is what makes these squares so interesting. Also, the coconut oil in the glaze definitely works much better than butter!

sticky mocha squares

30 g/⅓ cup cocoa powder
2 teaspoons bicarbonate of/
  baking soda
360 g/2 cups semolina/farina
¼ teaspoon salt
230 ml/1 cup plain soy yogurt
230 ml/1 cup plain soy milk
  (vanilla-flavoured or plain)
½ teaspoon apple cider
  vinegar
100 g/½ cup sunflower oil
195 g/¾ cup pure maple
  syrup
1 teaspoon coffee extract

For the glaze
100 g/½ cup coconut oil
170 ml/¾ cup non-dairy milk
100 g/3½ oz. vegan dark/
  bittersweet chocolate,
  finely chopped
¼ teaspoon bourbon vanilla
  powder
4 tablespoons brown rice
  or pure maple syrup
1 teaspoon coffee extract

*23 x 30-cm/9 x 12-in.
  baking pan, oiled*

Makes about 20

Preheat the oven to 180°C (350°F) Gas 4.

Sift together the cocoa powder and bicarbonate of/baking soda in a mixing bowl, then mix in the semolina/farina and salt.

In a separate bowl, whisk together the yogurt, milk, vinegar, oil, syrup and coffee extract. Pour into the bowl of dry ingredients and mix with a wooden spoon until combined.

Spoon the cake mixture into the prepared baking pan and spread level with a spatula. Bake in the preheated oven for 25 minutes.

Meanwhile, for the glaze, if the coconut oil has solidified, put the jar in a bowl of hot water until the oil has softened.

Heat the milk in a saucepan until hot but not boiling, then remove from the heat, add the chocolate and allow to melt. Stir until smooth.

Add the coconut oil, vanilla powder, syrup and coffee extract to the pan and whisk to get a smooth glaze. Keep warm until the cake has finished baking.

Pour the glaze over the hot cake in the pan and allow to cool completely. Most of the glaze will be absorbed by the cake and this is what makes it so moist.

Serve at room temperature on the day of baking if possible (or the next day), cut into slices.

These slices are a coconut-lover's heaven; they are creamy and rich, and the fluffy vanilla-flavoured frosting topped with loads of coconut and combined with a slightly crunchy base makes you wish for another portion, and another, and another…

raffaello slices

Preheat the oven to 160°C (325°F) Gas 3.

Sift together the flour, cornflour/cornstarch and baking powder in a mixing bowl, then mix in the salt, turmeric and coconut.

In a separate bowl, mix the oil, syrup, milk, vanilla extract and lemon juice or vinegar. Pour into the bowl of dry ingredients and mix gently with a spatula until combined.

Spoon the mixture evenly into the prepared baking pan, pressing it down lightly. This mixture is thicker than you might expect – it slightly resembles moist cookie dough. Put it in the preheated oven and check it after 10 minutes and every couple of minutes thereafter. Remove it from the oven as soon as you see a slight change in colour. If you wait until it gets golden brown, you might end up with a tasty but quite hard base that will be difficult to eat with a fork. When it is ready, remove it from the oven, allow it to cool for a couple of minutes, then cover it with clingfilm/plastic wrap to keep it soft. Allow to cool completely.

For the frosting, mix the cornflour/cornstarch into 120 ml/½ cup of the milk, then stir in the 2 tablespoons sugar, the vanilla powder and turmeric.

Heat the remaining milk in a saucepan until boiling, then remove from the heat and slowly add the cornflour/cornstarch mixture, whisking vigorously. Put back over low heat and whisk for a minute until the sticky cream starts bubbling. Remove from the heat, allow to cool completely and whisk until smooth again.

Very finely grind the remaining sugar in a spice mill or food processor. In a bowl, beat the margarine with an electric whisk until soft. Gradually add the powdered sugar and beat until light and fluffy. Now add the vanilla cream, gently mixing with a spatula to get an even, smooth frosting.

Spread the frosting evenly over the cooled base. Sprinkle the coconut over it to cover completely. Wrap in foil and refrigerate for a couple of hours before cutting into slices, to serve.

130 g/1 cup unbleached plain/all-purpose flour
2 tablespoons cornflour/cornstarch
1 teaspoon baking powder
a pinch of salt
a pinch of ground turmeric
55 g/⅔ cup desiccated coconut
100 g/½ cup sunflower oil
180 g/⅔ cup brown rice syrup
2 tablespoons plain soy milk
½ teaspoon vanilla extract
1 teaspoon lemon juice or apple cider vinegar

For the frosting
5 tablespoons cornflour/cornstarch
365 ml/1⅔ cups vanilla-flavoured soy milk
100 g/½ cup raw/unrefined brown sugar, plus 2 tablespoons
¼ teaspoon vanilla bourbon powder
a pinch of ground turmeric
100 g/¾ cup margarine, at room temperature
55 g/⅔ cup desiccated coconut, lightly toasted

24 x 17-cm/9½ x 7-in. baking pan, oiled

Makes about 24

I've been eating this dessert since I can remember and baking it since primary school. You can use nearly any seasonal produce and it will turn out tasty. I prefer using slightly sour fruit like sour cherries, cherry plums or apricots but it also works well with ripe peaches, apples and raspberries, for example. Frozen or canned fruit can also be used if you don't have any fresh fruit to hand.

fruit-topped bars

260 g/2 cups unbleached spelt flour
65 g/½ cup plain wholemeal/whole-wheat flour
1 teaspoon bicarbonate of/baking soda
1½ teaspoons baking powder
¼ teaspoon salt
¼ teaspoon bourbon vanilla powder
¼ teaspoon ground cinnamon
a few pinches of ground turmeric
80 g/½ cup hazelnuts or almonds, chopped
360 ml/1½ cups plain soy yogurt
170 g/⅔ cup pure maple syrup
100 g/½ cup coconut, safflower or other good-quality oil
freshly squeezed juice and grated zest of 1 lemon
1 teaspoon apple cider vinegar
350 g/2 cups pitted sour cherries or cherry plums

23 x 30-cm/9 x 12-in. baking pan, lined with parchment paper

Makes about 20

Preheat the oven to 180°C (350°F) Gas 4.

Sift together the flours, bicarbonate of/baking soda, baking powder, salt, vanilla powder, cinnamon and turmeric. Add the nuts and mix everything together.

In a separate bowl, mix the yogurt, syrup, oil, lemon juice and zest and vinegar. Pour into the bowl of dry ingredients and mix gently with a wooden spoon. Do not overmix.

Spoon the mixture into the prepared baking pan and spread level with a spatula.

Scatter the cherries or plums over the surface of the cake mixture, making sure there is some space between the fruit – you don't want to overload the cake with fruit otherwise it will turn out soggy.

Bake the cake in the preheated oven for about 35 minutes, or until golden brown. Remove from the oven and allow to cool in the pan.

Slice into squares and drizzle maple syrup over the top to serve.

At first, the idea of using cooked beans in a brownie mixture might not sound too promising or appealing. However, blended beans give a wonderful texture to the brownies and it's a great way to introduce plant protein to kids or people who wouldn't want to eat a bean stew for lunch. Cashews can be replaced by other nuts, but I suggest you try this wonderful combination; you won't be sorry!

bean and cashew brownies

If you want to cook the haricot/navy beans from scratch, soak 140 g/ ¾ cup dried beans in a lot of water overnight. Drain, cover with three times the volume of water and cook for 1 hour (or 40 minutes in a pressure cooker). Drain well.

Preheat the oven to 180°C (350°F) Gas 4.

Melt the chocolate in a heatproof bowl set over a saucepan of simmering water. Do not let the base of the bowl touch the water.

Put the melted chocolate, cooked beans, oil, syrup, lemon juice and zest in a food processor and blend until smooth.

If using whole cashews, finely grind them in a food processor or spice mill. Mix the flours, ground cashews, baking powder, salt and cinnamon in a mixing bowl. Add the bean mixture and fold in with a spatula until you get a smooth, thick consistency (much thicker than usual cake mixtures).

Spoon the cake mixture into the prepared baking pan and spread level with a spatula; if it sticks too much, wet it with warm water and try again. Bake in the preheated oven for 15–20 minutes. Do not overbake – they are supposed to be a little gooey! Allow to cool completely in the baking pan.

Cut into squares to serve. I like to serve them with a little homemade apricot jam which contrasts beautifully with the rich, heavy chocolate taste of these brownies.

300 g/2 cups canned unsalted haricot/navy beans (see method for an alternative)
200 g/1½ cups finely chopped vegan dark/bittersweet chocolate (70% cocoa)
65 g/⅓ cup sunflower oil
130 g/½ cup brown rice or pure maple syrup
freshly squeezed juice and grated zest of 1 lemon
80 g/½ cup whole or 80 g/ 1 cup finely ground cashews
85 g/⅔ cup unbleached plain/all-purpose flour
40 g/⅓ cup plain wholemeal/ whole-wheat flour
1 tablespoon baking powder
¼ teaspoon salt
¼ teaspoon ground cinnamon
2 tablespoons apricot jam, for serving

23 x 30-cm/9 x 12-in. baking pan, oiled

Makes about 20

These yummy treats do look funny – furry and white from all the coconut they have been rolled in! This is a recipe that I tried to "veganize" while still in high-school. It became quite popular and I know for a fact that it was the first cake a couple of my school friends attempted to make. So I assure you, you can make them too!

lamingtons

80 g/½ cup almonds or 80 g/
   1 cup ground almonds
260 g/2 cups unbleached
   plain/all-purpose flour
45 g/⅓ cup oat flour
1 tablespoon cornflour/
   cornstarch
1 teaspoon baking powder
1 teaspoon bicarbonate of/
   baking soda
¼ teaspoon salt
a pinch of saffron threads
100 g/½ cup safflower or
   sunflower oil
170 g/⅔ cup brown rice syrup
350 ml/1½ cups plain soy milk
1 teaspoon vanilla extract
160 g/2 cups desiccated
   coconut

For the glaze
300 ml/1⅓ cups non-dairy milk
50 g/⅓ cup non-hydrogenated
   margarine
70 g/½ cup finely chopped
   vegan dark/bittersweet
   chocolate
130 g/⅔ cup Demerara sugar

23 x 30-cm/9 x 12-in.
   baking pan, oiled

Makes 12

Preheat the oven to 180°C (350°F) Gas 4. Dust the baking pan with a little flour to coat the base and shake off any excess.

If using whole almonds, lightly roast them for a couple of minutes in the preheated oven, then finely grind them in a food processor or spice mill.

Sift the ground almonds, flours, cornflour/cornstarch, baking powder, bicarbonate of/baking soda and salt in a mixing bowl and stir in the saffron.

In a separate bowl, mix the oil, syrup, milk and vanilla extract. Pour into the bowl of dry ingredients and mix gently with a wooden spoon. Do not overmix.

Pour the mixture into the prepared baking pan and spread level with a spatula. Bake in the preheated oven for 20 minutes. Allow to cool completely in the pan, then cut into 12 squares.

Put the coconut on a big plate.

When the cake has cooled, for the glaze, put all ingredients in a saucepan over low heat and whisk occasionally until the margarine and chocolate have melted and the sugar has dissolved. Stir until smooth. Pour the hot glaze into a wide, shallow container or a small baking pan. Dip each cooled cake square into it, waiting for it to soak up some of the glaze all over before taking it out with a fork. Don't be impatient – if you just dip the squares in too quickly, you'll have a lot of glaze left and the lamingtons won't be moist.

Use a clean fork to roll each square in the coconut. Try to do it neatly as the glaze can stick to the coconut and your squares won't look nice and white.

Allow to cool before serving. If you do happen to have some glaze left, drizzle it over each square before serving. Enjoy!

Home-baked bars are so easy to make and you'll be very grateful to find them in your cupboard whenever you crave sweets or need a takeaway breakfast or healthy snack. Kids love to get these in their lunchboxes and grandmas love to dip them into warm soy milk after their afternoon nap (well, at least lactose-intolerant grandmas like mine!). Use any syrup you have available; agave, rice, maple, apple, date – they all work well in this recipe.

oat bars filled with jam

Preheat the oven to 180°C (350°F) Gas 4.

Mix the oats, flour, vanilla powder, cinnamon, baking powder and salt in a mixing bowl, then add the syrup and oil and mix thoroughly with a wooden spoon.

Spoon half the dough into the prepared baking pan and press down evenly into the pan. Spread the fruit preserve over the dough with a wet spatula, then spoon over the remaining dough, smoothing the top with a spatula.

Bake in the preheated oven for 20 minutes. Remove from the baking pan and allow to cool on a wire rack.

Cut into squares to serve. Refrigerated, they'll keep for 2 weeks in an airtight container but it's more likely they'll be gone in 2 days!

VARIATION: You could also try filling these with hazelnut or carob spread.

300 g/3 cups rolled oats
130 g/1 cup unbleached spelt flour
½ teaspoon bourbon vanilla powder
½ teaspoon ground cinnamon
1 teaspoon baking powder
½ teaspoon salt
170 g/⅔ cup brown rice syrup (see Introduction above)
130 g/½ cup coconut or sunflower oil
90 g/4 tablespoons naturally sweetened fruit jam

23 x 30-cm/9 x 12-inch baking pan, greased

Makes 12

CHAPTER 4

Cookies & biscuits

For the cookie jar, a surprise visit from a friend, a late-night snack or to accompany a cup of coffee – it needn't take long to whip up a batch of bite-size cookies and biscuits to munch on throughout the week. Whether you keep them simple and wholesome, or a little more refined with a drizzle of chocolate, it's up to you!

As the mums of all my best friends know I love baking, I occasionally get emails from them with interesting recipes for their favourite desserts. Although they always contain milk, butter and lots of sugar, they always inspire me and I often end up making a vegan version that everybody likes even more than the original! The same story goes for these apricot and chocolate bites; the Krpan family were kind enough to reveal a similar recipe that has since become a part of my sweet repertoire too.

apricot and chocolate bites

Preheat the oven to 160°C (325°F) Gas 3.

Put the apricots, orange juice and zest and ginger in a small saucepan over medium heat. Heat until hot but not boiling. Remove from the heat and transfer to a food processor. Blend to a paste but don't worry if a few chunks remain.

Put the coconut in a heavy frying pan and toast over medium–low heat, stirring occasionally, until pale golden – about 8 minutes. Do not burn! Remove from the pan and allow to cool slightly.

Mix the flour and salt in a bowl and add the toasted coconut.

If the coconut oil has solidified, put the jar in a bowl of hot water until the oil has softened. Add it to the apricot paste with the syrup and mix well. Now add this to the dry ingredients in the bowl and mix with a wooden spoon until well incorporated.

Use a small spoon to scoop portions of dough onto the prepared baking sheets. Shape into balls, then flatten slightly with the back of the spoon. You should get about 32–35 cookies.

Bake the cookies in batches in the preheated oven for 10–12 minutes, just until lightly golden. If you overbake them, they will become tough. Allow to cool for a couple of minutes, then transfer to a wire rack to cool completely.

Melt the chocolate in a heatproof bowl set over a saucepan of simmering water. Do not let the base of the bowl touch the water. Add the oil and stir until smooth, then allow to cool slightly.

Dip each cookie halfway into the melted chocolate. Allow to cool and set completely before serving. Store in an airtight container for up to 2 weeks

100 g/⅔ cup unsulfured dried
    apricots, chopped
freshly squeezed juice and
    grated zest of 1 big orange
¼ teaspoon ground ginger
80 g/1 cup desiccated coconut
150 g/1 cup plus
    2 tablespoons unbleached
    plain/all-purpose flour
¼ teaspoon salt
100 g/½ cup coconut oil
70 g/¼ cup brown rice or
    other syrup
50 g/⅓ cup finely chopped
    vegan dark/bittersweet
    chocolate
¼ teaspoon sunflower oil

*baking sheets, lined with
    parchment paper*

Makes 32–35

Almost all cookie recipes (at least the ones that I make) are very simple; you can have a freshly baked batch in less than 30 minutes, and these are no exception. The mix of spices makes them more of a winter choice, but feel free to use other spices, or omit them – it won't change their crunchiness or yumminess at all!

spicy oat cookies with cashews

100 g/1 cup rolled oats
160 g/1 cup cashews
130 g/1 cup unbleached plain/all-purpose flour
¼ teaspoon baking powder
½ teaspoon ground cinnamon
¼ teaspoon ground nutmeg
¼ teaspoon ground ginger
a pinch of chilli powder (optional)
¼ teaspoon salt
130 g/½ cup pure maple syrup
100 g/½ cup coconut or sunflower oil
1 tablespoon ground flaxseeds

baking sheets, lined with parchment paper

Makes about 30

Preheat the oven to 180°C (350°F) Gas 4.

Coarsely grind the oats in a food processor or spice mill. Finely grind the cashews in the same way.

Sift the flour, baking powder, cinnamon, nutmeg, ginger, chilli powder and salt in a bowl, then stir in the ground oats and cashews. Mix well.

Put the syrup, oil and flaxseeds in a separate bowl and whisk vigorously. Pour into the bowl of dry ingredients and mix with a wooden spoon.

Pull off walnut-sized pieces of dough and roll into balls. Arrange on the baking sheets about 3 cm/1¼ inches apart. Gently flatten each ball with the help of an oiled spatula or fish slice.

Bake the cookies in batches in the preheated oven for 10–12 minutes, and take them out as soon as the bottoms turn slightly golden. Don't worry if they seem soft – they will harden as they cool down.

Remove from the oven, transfer to a wire rack and allow to cool. Store in an airtight container for up to 2 weeks.

One day, as I was getting ready to bake a batch of cookies and was reaching for ingredients in my cupboard, a jar of couscous wouldn't get out of my way… It was obvious I had to use couscous in the cookie dough, so I did. And look what I created! This is a great cookie with a crunchy texture, a maple aroma and a slightly soft centre filled with jam. I cannot think of a better way to use up some of the plum jam that I make in the summer to enjoy throughout the year.

couscous and jam crunchies

Preheat the oven to 180°C (350°F) Gas 4.

Put the couscous, almonds, flour, flaxseeds, vanilla powder and salt in a mixing bowl and mix.

Put the syrup, oil and almond extract in a separate bowl and whisk vigorously. Pour into the bowl of dry ingredients and mix with a wooden spoon.

Pull off walnut-sized pieces of dough and roll into balls. Flatten them between your palms until 1 cm/½ inch thick. Arrange them on the baking sheets spaced just slightly apart – they won't spread during baking.

Now use the bottom of a teaspoon, or even better, a teaspoon-sized measuring spoon to gently press a hole in the middle of each cookie. Make circle motions to widen the hole, but don't press too hard otherwise you might break through the bottom of the cookie. Fill each hole with a full teaspoon of jam. Bake in the preheated oven for 15–16 minutes. Don't worry if they seem soft – they will harden as they cool down.

Remove from the oven and allow to cool on the baking sheets. Store in an airtight container for up to 2 weeks.

120 g/¾ cup couscous
160 g/1¾ cups ground almonds
130 g/1 cup unbleached plain/all-purpose flour
1 tablespoon ground flaxseeds
¼ teaspoon bourbon vanilla powder
¼ teaspoon salt
130 g/½ cup pure maple syrup
100 g/½ cup sunflower oil
½ teaspoon almond extract
24 teaspoons/200 g/⅔ cup plum or other thick, naturally sweetened jam

baking sheets, lined with parchment paper

Makes about 24

There are people who love coconut, and there are those who don't. I personally cannot understand what there is not to like! Coconut is just so wonderful in all its forms and I get jealous of people living in countries where you can buy young coconuts, drink the water, use up the flesh in smoothies and enjoy its wonderful taste and texture. But then I bake these cookies and I'm happy that desiccated coconut is a product available in many stores, wherever I am!

my favourite coconut cookies

130 g/1 cup unbleached spelt or unbleached plain/ all-purpose flour

¼ teaspoon bicarbonate of/ baking soda

¼ teaspoon salt

¼ teaspoon vanilla bourbon powder

160 g/2 cups desiccated coconut

75 g/⅓ cup coconut or soy milk

135 g/⅔ cup Demerara sugar

65 g/⅓ cup coconut or sunflower oil

1 tablespoon ground flaxseeds (optional)

50 g/⅓ cup finely chopped vegan dark/bittersweet chocolate

baking sheet, lined with parchment paper

Makes about 20

Preheat the oven to 180°C (350°F) Gas 4.

Sift together the flour, bicarbonate of/baking soda, salt and vanilla powder in a bowl, then stir in the desiccated coconut.

Put the milk, sugar, oil and flaxseeds, if using, in a separate bowl and whisk vigorously until well combined. Pour into the bowl of dry ingredients and mix with a spatula until you get dough that is firm but a little sticky – it shouldn't be dry or crumbly.

Wet your hands and pull off a tablespoon of the dough. You can either roll it into a ball and flatten it between your palms to get a flat, round cookie, or, what I do is roll the tablespoon of dough into a sausage and then flatten it into a flat oval. That makes them easier to dip into tea or hot cocoa. Also, ovals are convenient if you like writing chocolate messages on cookies, and I do that often!

Continue with the rest of the dough, arranging each cookie 2 cm/ ¾ inch apart on the prepared baking sheet. Bake in the preheated oven for 8–10 minutes, no longer! Take them out as soon as the bottoms turn slightly golden. Don't worry if they seem pale and a little soft – they will harden as they cool down.

Remove the cookies from the oven, transfer to a wire rack and allow to cool completely.

Melt the chocolate in a heatproof bowl set over a saucepan of simmering water. Do not let the base of the bowl touch the water. Drizzle the melted chocolate over the cooled cookies and allow to set. Store in an airtight container for up to 2 weeks.

Japanese persimmon or kaki is a sweet fruit with a soft texture. It is a species native to China but is now widely spread throughout the Mediterranean too. Beautiful persimmon trees laden with fruits can often be seen in gardens in Istria. I always allow the fruits to ripen and soften after the harvest – this brings out their best flavour.

drop cookies with persimmon and cranberries

Preheat the oven to 180°C (350°F) Gas 4.

In a large mixing bowl, beat together the coconut oil or margarine, the syrup and persimmon pulp. Add the walnuts and cranberries and stir through. Sift the flours, baking powder, cinnamon and salt into the bowl and stir in with a wooden spoon. If the dough seems too dry, add a splash of milk but not too much – the dough should be thick enough not to slide off the spoon.

Drop generous tablespoons of the dough onto the prepared baking sheets, about 1 cm/½ inch apart. Bake the cookies in the preheated oven for 15 minutes.

Remove the cookies from the oven and allow to cool on the baking sheets. Store in an airtight container for up to 2 weeks.

70 g/½ cup coconut oil
  or non-hydrogenated
  margarine, at room
  temperature
170 g/⅔ cup brown rice syrup
250 ml/1 cup persimmon pulp
  from 1–2 persimmons),
  pushed through a sieve/
  strainer
60 g/½ cup chopped walnuts
60 g/½ cup dried cranberries
200 g/1½ cups unbleached
  plain/all-purpose flour
60 g/½ cup unbleached
  spelt or plain wholemeal/
  whole-wheat flour
2 teaspoons baking powder
½ teaspoon ground cinnamon
¼ teaspoon salt
plain soy milk, as needed

baking sheets, lined with
  parchment paper

Makes about 26

My dad adores this treat and he asked me to include it in this cookbook so other people can enjoy it too. Originally, the recipe called for a lot of sugar and many eggs, but the vegan version is so much healthier and tastes even better! Just make sure that the temperature of the ingredients for the dough is right (everything ice-cold!) otherwise the base could turn out crumbly or oily.

dad's hazelnut triangles

½ quantity Sweet Pie Dough (page 20)

For the hazelnut topping
50 g/⅓ cup non-hydrogenated margarine
240 g/1½ cups chopped hazelnuts
50 g/½ cup ground hazelnuts
6 tablespoons non-dairy milk
100 g/½ cup Demerara sugar
¼ teaspoon bourbon vanilla powder
2 tablespoons arrowroot powder or cornflour/ cornstarch
1 teaspoon rum
a pinch of salt

23 x 30-cm/9 x 12-in. baking pan

Makes 24

Make and refrigerate the Sweet Pie Dough as described on page 20. Allow the dough to rest at room temperature for 5–10 minutes before rolling it out.

Preheat the oven to 180°C (350°F) Gas 4.

For the hazelnut topping, melt the margarine in a large saucepan over low heat, then remove from the heat and add the chopped and ground hazelnuts, milk, sugar, vanilla powder, arrowroot, rum and salt. Whisk vigorously.

Place the dough on a sheet of lightly floured parchment paper, dust with a little flour and roll it out to fit the base of the baking pan – about 23 x 30 cm/9 x 12 inches. Brush off any excess flour and transfer the dough, together with the parchment paper, into the pan and prick it all over with a fork. Bake in the preheated oven for 8 minutes. Leave the oven on.

Remove the pan from the oven and spread the hazelnut topping evenly over the baked base with a spatula.

Put back in the oven and bake for 20–22 minutes, or until starting to turn golden. Don't worry if the topping feels a little soft – it has to cool completely before you can cut it. The best idea is to refrigerate it for a couple of hours.

To serve, cut the cold bake into 24 triangles with a sharp knife. If you try to cut it when it's still warm, the topping will crumble and you'll end up having to eat it with a spoon, so be patient! Serve it with a cup of tea or non-dairy latte. Store in an airtight container for up to 2 weeks.

Vegan biscotti? Yes, it's possible to make them in spite of the fact that the main ingredient holding everything together in conventional biscotti recipes is egg white. Follow my instructions precisely and don't fear, these are even better than the same old regular biscotti! You can use any nuts and spices instead of pistachios and fennel seeds, or try adding a small amount of dried fruit to the mix.

pistachio and fennel biscotti

Preheat the oven to 180°C (350°F) Gas 4.

Sift together the flour, baking powder, bicarbonate of/baking soda, salt, arrowroot, vanilla powder and turmeric in a large bowl. Stir in the fennel seeds and pistachios.

In a separate bowl, whisk together the milk, oil, sugar and lemon juice and zest. Pour into the dry ingredients and stir well with a wooden spoon to form a soft dough that sticks lightly to your fingers. Turn the dough out onto the prepared baking sheet, and, with the help of a silicone spatula, form 2 logs about 27 x 6 cm/ 10½ x 2½ inches, neatening the edges and ends. Bake in the preheated oven for 20 minutes, or until lightly golden. Allow to cool completely on the baking sheet. Don't skip this step otherwise the biscotti slices will crumble.

Preheat the oven to 150°C (300°F) Gas 2.

Place the biscotti logs on a chopping/cutting board and use a sharp bread knife to cut them, at an angle, into 1-cm/½-inch thick slices. Lay them down carefully on the lined baking sheet. Rebake for 10–20 minutes, turning the slices over halfway through baking, depending on how crisp you want them. Allow to cool completely on the baking sheet.

Store in a big, long cookie jar hidden at the back of the most remote kitchen cupboard otherwise they'll be gone in a minute! They will keep for up to 2 weeks. Serve with a cup of non-dairy latte or fennel tea!

200 g/1½ cups unbleached plain/all-purpose flour
½ teaspoon baking powder
½ teaspoon bicarbonate of/ baking soda
¼ teaspoon salt (omit if using salted pistachios)
2 tablespoons arrowroot powder or cornflour/ cornstarch
⅛ teaspoon bourbon vanilla powder
a pinch of ground turmeric
½–1 tablespoon fennel seeds
260 g/2 cups shelled pistachios (raw, unsalted, if available)
80 ml/⅓ cup plain soy milk
65 g/⅓ cup sunflower oil
100 g/½ cup Demerara sugar
freshly squeezed juice and grated zest of 1 lemon

baking sheet, lined with parchment paper

Makes about 20

Even though I don't drink coffee, coffee-flavoured treats immediately go onto my favourite foods list. You can use cocoa powder instead of ground cocoa beans here, but I prefer grinding the beans in a coffee grinder myself – their texture very much resembles freshly ground coffee beans, which is so appropriate for this recipe. The icing gives an additional sweet coffee kick for your taste buds!

coffee toffee cookies

30 g/⅓ cup raw cocoa beans
   (or nibs) or 30 g/⅓ cup
   cocoa powder
100 g/½ cup coconut oil
100 g/½ cup Demerara sugar
60 ml/¼ cup plain soy milk
2 teaspoons coffee extract
¼ teaspoon apple cider
   vinegar
200 g/1½ cups unbleached
   spelt flour
½ teaspoon baking powder
1 tablespoon ground
   flaxseeds
¼ teaspoon bourbon vanilla
   powder
2 tablespoons ground
   almonds
¼ teaspoon salt
¼ teaspoon ground cinnamon
chopped nuts, for sprinkling

For the icing
65 g/⅓ cup Demerara sugar
1 tablespoon cornflour/
   cornstarch
2 tablespoons plain soy milk
1 teaspoon coffee extract

*baking sheets, lined with
   parchment paper*

Makes 25

Preheat the oven to 180°C (350°F) Gas 4.

If using cocoa beans, grind them in a coffee or spice grinder to a fine powder.

If the coconut oil has solidified, put the jar in a bowl of hot water until the oil has softened. Whisk together the oil, sugar, milk, coffee extract and vinegar.

In a separate bowl, sift together the flour and baking powder, then stir in the flaxseeds, vanilla powder, ground almonds, salt and cinnamon. Tip into the bowl of wet ingredients and mix into a smooth dough with a spatula.

Divide the dough into 25 and roll into balls. Arrange them on the prepared baking sheets about 2 cm/¾ inch apart. Gently flatten each ball with the back of a spoon, trying to avoid making cracks. Bake in the preheated oven for 9–10 minutes. Do not overbake them – they should still be a little soft. Allow to cool completely on the baking sheets.

For the icing, it's better to finely grind the sugar in a coffee or spice grinder, but you can also try without grinding it. Mix the cornflour/cornstarch into the milk in a heatproof bowl. Add the coffee extract and sugar and mix. Set over a saucepan of simmering water (do not let the base of the bowl touch the water) and whisk well for a couple of minutes to allow the starch to thicken slightly over the steam. Remove from the heat, then allow to cool for 10 minutes.

Spoon some icing over each cold cookie and sprinkle chopped nuts over the top. Allow to set for at least 1 hour after which the icing shouldn't be sticky, but smooth and firm to the touch.

Store in an airtight container at room temperature, or, in the summer months, in the fridge. They will keep for up to 2 weeks.

CHAPTER 5

Pies, tarts & strudels

For an alternative to a birthday cake, a wintry, warming dessert, a celebration of summer fruit or a slice of comfort after a long day – these recipes come in all shapes, sizes and characters to suit all sorts of needs. Going vegan needn't mean the end of pastry and these pies, tarts and strudels show how much there is to enjoy.

Apple pie must be one of the most baked desserts in my family's kitchen! Pies in general are very popular, but this combination of crumbly crust and the lovely smell and taste of apples combined with cinnamon and raisins is an irresistible and irreplaceable year-round treat! I often bake pies in rectangular baking pans and serve them dusted with little icing/confectioners'-sugar-and-cinnamon, but you could serve yours with vegan custard if you prefer.

european-style apple pie

Make the Sweet Pie Dough as described on page 20 but just before refrigerating it, divide it in half; one part should be slightly bigger than the other. Shape each portion into a disc, wrap in clingfilm/plastic wrap and refrigerate it for at least 1 hour, and up to 2 days. If you're in a hurry you can chill the larger portion of dough in the freezer for 15 minutes and the smaller one just until you're ready to use it. If refrigerated, allow the dough to rest at room temperature for 5–10 minutes before rolling it out.

Preheat the oven to 180°C (350°F) Gas 4.

Cut out a piece of parchment paper to fit the base of the baking pan. Dust with a little flour and place the larger portion of dough on it, then dust the dough with flour. Roll out with a rolling pin, from the centre outwards, until it's roughly the size of the base of the pan. Brush off any excess flour and transfer the dough, together with the paper, into the pan. If necessary, use a glass to roll out the dough so that it covers the entire base of the pan. Prick all over with a fork and bake in the preheated oven for 6–7 minutes. Leave the oven on.

For the filling, grate the apples by hand with a grater, or core them and use a food processor to grate them. If the apples are very juicy, squeeze out some of the juice to prevent it seeping into the dough and making it soggy. Mix the apples with the raisins, syrup and cinnamon, then spread over the half-baked base with a spatula.

Take the smaller portion of dough and grate by hand with a grater. Scatter it evenly over the apple filling. Put back in the oven and bake for 25–35 minutes, until the top is golden and the base is also nice and golden (lift the paper with a spatula to check this).

Allow to cool in the pan before serving. Store in an airtight container for a couple of days.

Sweet Pie Dough (page 20)

For the filling
1.5 kg/3½ lb. apples, peeled
60 g/½ cup raisins
65 g/¼ cup brown rice syrup
½ teaspoon ground cinnamon

40 x 28-cm/16 x 11-in. baking pan (for a thinner crust) or 23 x 30 cm/9 x 12-in. baking pan (for a thicker crust)

Serves about 9

I was surprised to find so many different types of cheesecake around the world! Some are unbaked, some are baked; some are fruit flavoured, others contain chocolate. My vegan cheesecake is baked and apricot flavoured, with a pie crust, and it looks beautiful!

apricot and tofu cheesecake

½ quantity **Sweet Pie Dough**
    (page 20)

For the tofu cream
500 g/1 lb. 2 oz. plain,
    medium-soft tofu
100 g/scant ½ cup vanilla soy
    custard
1½ tablespoons non-
    hydrogenated margarine
85 g/⅓ cup rice or agave
    syrup
freshly squeezed juice of
    1½ lemons
grated zest of 2 lemons
1 tablespoon unbleached
    plain/all-purpose flour
4–5 ripe firm apricots (if in
    season), pitted and sliced

For the apricot jelly
1 teaspoon agar powder or
    2 teaspoons agar flakes
110 ml/½ cup apple
    concentrate
135 g/½ cup smooth, naturally
    sweetened apricot jam

*28-cm/11-in. springform cake
    pan or loose-based tart pan*

Serves 6–8

Make and refrigerate the Sweet Pie Dough as described on page 20.

For the tofu cream, blanch the tofu in boiling water for 2 minutes. Put it in a food processor with the custard, margarine, syrup, lemon juice and zest, and flour. Blend until smooth.

Preheat the oven to 180°C (350°F) Gas 4.

Take the dough out of the fridge. Place it between 2 sheets of parchment paper and use a rolling pin to roll the dough out to a circle about 31 cm/13 inches in diameter. Loosely roll the dough circle around the rolling pin and unroll it over the tart pan. Neatly line the pan with the dough and trim off any excess from the edges with a pastry wheel or your fingers. Patch up any holes with dough off-cuts. Prick the base all over with a fork and bake in the preheated oven for 8–10 minutes. Leave the oven on.

Remove the pan from the oven and pour the tofu cream into the tart crust. Spread level with a spatula. Put back in the oven and bake for 20 minutes, or until the tofu cream starts turning very lightly golden. Allow to cool completely in the pan. Arrange the apricot slices over the cooled tofu cream, if using.

For the apricot jelly, put 285 ml/1¼ cups water, the agar, apple concentrate and jam in a saucepan and bring to the boil, whisking occasionally. Lower the heat and cook for 2 minutes if you are using agar powder, or 8 minutes if using flakes or until the flakes have completely melted.

Gently ladle the hot jelly over the cooled cheesecake but if you think it will leak over the edges, only ladle some of it in, then wait for 3–4 minutes to firm slightly before adding the rest. Allow to cool completely. This is best done in the fridge.

Cut into slices with a sharp knife dipped in hot water.

When peaches are in season, I can eat huge amounts of them every day, but instead of eating them raw all the time, I use them to bake fancy summer desserts once in a while. It's especially nice to serve this crumble on a stormy summer evening when there is a bit of rain and wind and everybody feels very shivery and miserable even though it's summertime!

peach crumble

Preheat the oven to 150°C (300°F) Gas 2.

For the crumble, put the nuts in a baking pan and roast them in the preheated oven for 8–10 minutes. Rub off any skins that have loosened from the nuts, then roughly chop the nuts by hand or in a food processor. Big pieces will burn while the crumble is baking, so make them quite small.

Put the flour, oats, zest, cinnamon, vanilla powder and salt in a bowl and stir. Add the syrup and mix well, then work the margarine in with your hands, rubbing it quickly between your fingers. When the mixture looks crumbly, add the chopped nuts.

Preheat the oven to 180°C (350°F) Gas 4.

Blanch the peaches in a saucepan of boiling water for 1–2 minutes – just long enough to be able to peel the skin off easily. Transfer them to a bowl of cold water so you don't burn your fingers, then peel off the skin. Halve and pit the peaches and cut them into wedges. Toss them with the apple juice concentrate, flour and salt. Spread them in the ovenproof dish and cover them evenly with the crumble.

Bake in the preheated oven for about 35 minutes or until the crumble topping is golden brown and the juice is bubbling up around the edges.

The crumble is best served warm, but if you happen to have leftovers and serve it as a dessert the next day, I'm sure no one will complain!

1.8 kg/about 8 firm but
  ripe peaches
2–3 tablespoons apple juice
  concentrate
1 tablespoon unbleached
  plain/all-purpose flour
a pinch of salt

For the crumble
80 g/½ cup hazelnuts
  or other nuts
65 g/½ cup unbleached
  plain/all-purpose flour
50 g/½ cup rolled oats
grated zest of 1 orange
  or lemon
¼ teaspoon ground cinnamon
⅛ teaspoon bourbon vanilla
  powder
a pinch of salt
85 g/⅓ cup brown rice or
  agave syrup
50 g/⅓ cup non-hydrogenated
  margarine, at room
  temperature

ovenproof dish, 8-cup capacity

Serves 6–8

Here is a very rustic-looking, freeform tart that I cannot resist eating more of than I should! Using non-hydrogenated margarine in this type of dough is a little tricky; it will result in a healthier dessert that will impress with its taste but maybe not with its looks! If you prefer it to be prettier, use shortening instead. I love it just the way it is.

plum crostata

3 tablespoons pure maple syrup, for brushing

For the crust (see method before starting)
100 g/¾ cup unbleached plain/all-purpose flour
65 g/½ cup plain wholemeal/whole-wheat flour
¼ teaspoon salt
70 g/½ cup non-hydrogenated margarine
1 tablespoon pure maple syrup
ice-cold water, if needed

For the filling
350 g/12 oz. small plums, eg. Italian prune plums
2 tablespoons naturally sweetened plum (or other) jam
grated zest of 1 lemon
2 tablespoons pure maple syrup (optional)
35 g/⅓ cup ground almonds or other nuts
¼ teaspoon ground cinnamon

Serves 4–5

For the crust, refrigerate all the ingredients (but freeze the margarine) for 30 minutes before starting.

After 30 minutes, put the flours and salt in a bowl and stir. Gradually add small pieces of margarine to the bowl and using a fork (or a food processor), mix them in until the ingredients look crumbly. Add the syrup and mix in with a spatula. Now check – if the dough just holds together, it's ready. If it's too dry, add 1 teaspoon ice-cold water, mix in and check again. You should get a dough that is not falling apart but isn't sticky or moist. Don't overwork it and don't handle it too much.

Shape the dough into a disc, wrap in clingfilm/plastic wrap and refrigerate it for at least 1 hour, and up to 3 days.

Meanwhile, for the filling, pit and quarter the plums. Mix them with the jam, zest and syrup, if using.

Preheat the oven to 180°C (350°F) Gas 4.

Take the dough out of the fridge. Place it between 2 sheets of parchment paper and use a rolling pin to roll the dough out to a circle about 28 cm/11 inches in diameter. Discard the top sheet of paper. Transfer the dough, together with the bottom sheet of paper, to a baking sheet. Sprinkle the ground almonds and cinnamon evenly over the dough. Spoon the filling over this, leaving a 4-cm/1¾-inch border. Fold the border over to encase the filling around the edge. Do this gently, and if the dough crumbles or cracks a little, don't worry, just try to patch it up by pressing lightly with your fingertips. It will come together during baking. Brush maple syrup around the edge of the crostata and bake in the preheated oven for 25–30 minutes.

Allow to cool completely on the baking sheet before cutting into slices to serve.

Not all baked desserts must have baked fillings. Why not contrast the crumbly crust with some fresh, raw fruit for extra freshness and flavour? Made with olive oil, these tartlets are quite light, and the crust is neutral so it can be used to make savoury tartlets as well. Using a muffin pan to bake them is very practical, so you don't need to buy mini-tart pans just for this recipe!

fresh fruit tartlets

For the crust, sift together the flour, cornmeal, baking powder and salt in a bowl. Whisk in the oil, lemon juice and ice-cold water. Knead the dough for a few seconds, just until it holds together. Add a couple more drops of water if it seems too dry. Wrap in clingfilm/plastic wrap and refrigerate for at least 1 hour.

Meanwhile, for the filling, slice or chop the fruit into small pieces and mix them with the jam, vanilla powder, rum and salt.

Preheat the oven to 180°C (350°F) Gas 4.

Take the dough out of the fridge. Divide into 8 equal portions and place each in a hole of the muffin pan. Press and pat the dough gently to line the base and reach halfway up the sides. Make sure the layer of dough in the base is quite thin as it rises a bit during baking, and you will want some space inside the tartlet case later for the fruit. Prick the base of each case with a fork and bake in the preheated oven for 12–15 minutes, or until lightly golden. Do not overbake. Allow to cool completely before carefully turning the cases out of the pan with a spatula or a small knife.

Just before serving, put a tablespoon of custard, if using, inside each tartlet case and top with as much fruit as it can take. Decorate with fresh herbs and drizzle over and around with maple syrup.

fresh mint, melissa or mini-basil leaves, for decoration
pure maple syrup, for drizzling

For the crust
215 g/1⅔ cups unbleached plain/all-purpose flour
2 tablespoons fine cornmeal
½ teaspoon baking powder
¼ teaspoon sea salt
100 g/½ cup olive oil
1 teaspoon lemon juice
1 tablespoon ice-cold water

For the filling
300 g/10 oz. seasonal fruits, (the combination of apricots and nectarines is nice)
140 g/½ cup naturally sweetened apricot jam
¼ teaspoon bourbon vanilla powder
1 teaspoon rum or mirin
a pinch of salt
8 tablespoons vanilla soy custard (optional)

muffin pan

Makes 8 tartlets

Ganache is usually made with cream but I use soft tofu instead and the result is smooth and rich, making a great tart filling. I created this recipe with serious chocoholics in mind, adding chocolate mousse on top of the ganache.

chocolate ganache tart

½ quantity Sweet Pie Dough (page 20)

For the ganache
620 g/1 lb. 6 oz. plain, soft tofu
390 g/3 cups finely chopped vegan dark/bittersweet chocolate (70% cocoa)
grated zest of 2½ lemons
brown rice syrup or other sweetener, to taste
non-dairy milk or cream, if needed

For the mousse
450 ml/2 cups chocolate soy or oat milk
160 g/1¼ cups finely chopped vegan dark/bittersweet chocolate (70% cocoa)
85 g/⅓ cup brown rice syrup
90 g/7 tablespoons cornflour/ cornstarch

28-cm/11-in. springform cake pan or loose-based tart pan

Serves 6–8

Make and refrigerate the Sweet Pie Dough as described on page 20.

For the ganache, blanch the tofu in boiling water for 2 minutes. Meanwhile, melt the chocolate in a heatproof bowl set over a saucepan of simmering water. Do not let the base of the bowl touch the water. Put the blanched tofu, melted chocolate and lemon zest in food processor. Blend until smooth. Taste and if it's not sweet enough, blend in syrup to taste; if too thick, add a little milk or cream while blending.

Preheat the oven to 180°C (350°F) Gas 4.

Take the dough out of the fridge. Place it between 2 sheets of parchment paper and use a rolling pin to roll the dough out to a circle about 31 cm/ 13 inches in diameter. Loosely roll the dough circle around the rolling pin and unroll it over the tart pan. Neatly line the pan with the dough and trim off any excess from the edges with a pastry wheel or your fingers. Patch up any holes with dough off-cuts. Prick the base all over with a fork and bake in the preheated oven for 8–10 minutes. Leave the oven on.

Remove the pan from the oven and pour the ganache into the tart crust. Spread level with a spatula. Put back in the oven and bake for 15 minutes or until the edges turn lightly golden. Allow to cool completely in the pan.

For the mousse, heat the chocolate milk in a saucepan, then add the chocolate and syrup and whisk until the chocolate has melted. Mix the cornflour/cornstarch into 5–6 tablespoons water. Slowly add this to the saucepan over low heat, whisking vigorously. Keep whisking and it will start to thicken once it reaches the right temperature. Allow to cool slightly.

Spread the mousse over the cold ganache in the tart case with the spatula. Refrigerate but allow to come to room temperature for 20 minutes before serving. Cut into slices with a sharp knife dipped in hot water.

Fruit strudels are wonderful! Made healthily with little oil and healthy sweeteners, they can be eaten as a dessert, for breakfast, packed in lunchboxes or picnic baskets. This is a nice autumn combination of sweet pears and untreated (unsulfured) dried apricots with a touch of rum, vanilla and citrus aroma.

aromatic pear strudel

Take the filo/phyllo sheets out of the fridge 30 minutes before making the strudel. This will prevent the sheets from cracking during baking.

Meanwhile, put the apricots in a bowl with the rum, vanilla extract, lemon juice and zest and allow to soak while you prepare the pears, or longer if possible.

Preheat the oven to 180°C (350°F) Gas 4.

Peel and core the pears. Cut them into small cubes and mix them with the soaked apricots and the apple concentrate or syrup. Divide the mixture into 5 equal portions.

Place a sheet of filo/phyllo on a dry work surface with the longer side facing you. (Cover the remaining sheets with clingfilm/plastic wrap to prevent them from drying out.) Brush the coconut-oil mixture lightly over the sheet. Cover it with another sheet (this one doesn't need oiling).

Spread one portion of pears lengthwise along the bottom edge of the sheet. Arrange them in a 6-cm/2½-inch-wide strip, leaving a 2-cm/¾-inch edge on each side to prevent the filling from spilling out. Roll the sheet up carefully around the filling and into a nice strudel and place in the baking pan. Repeat with the remaining sheets and filling to get 5 strudels in the pan. Brush them lightly with the coconut-oil mixture and use a sharp knife to score each strudel into 4 slices.

Bake the strudel in the preheated oven for 25–30 minutes or until golden.

Serve warm or cold. It will keep in an airtight container in the fridge for up to 3 days and should be reheated in the oven before serving. If you serve it with vegan vanilla custard, you will be adored by your family and guests!

500 g/1 lb. 2 oz./10 large sheets of filo/phyllo pastry
125 g/15 unsulfured dried apricots, chopped
2 tablespoons rum or mirin
2 teaspoons vanilla extract
freshly squeezed juice and grated zest of 2 lemons or oranges
a pinch of salt
8 ripe pears, eg. Abate
85 g/⅓ cup apple juice concentrate or pure maple syrup
65 g/¼ cup coconut oil mixed with 4 tablespoons water

40 x 28-cm/16 x 11-in. baking pan, lightly oiled

Makes 20 slices

This is a vegan version of a traditional dessert from the northern border between Croatia and Slovenia, originally called 'gibanica'.

apple, poppy-seed and walnut pie

500 g/1 lb. 2 oz./12 sheets of filo/phyllo pastry
100 g/½ cup sunflower oil

For the poppy-seed layer
400 ml/1¾ cups non-dairy milk
200 g/2⅓ cups ground poppy seeds (available online)
5 tablespoons brown rice syrup
40 g/3 tablespoons raisins
¼ teaspoon bourbon vanilla powder
1 tablespoon rum
grated zest of 1 lemon

For the tofu layer
400 g/14 oz. fresh, plain, medium-soft tofu
2 tablespoons arrowroot powder or cornflour/cornstarch
110 ml/½ cup non-dairy milk
55 ml/⅓ cup lemon juice
3 tablespoons brown rice syrup

For the walnut layer
200 g/1¼ cups walnuts
30 g/⅓ cup fine breadcrumbs
5 tablespoons brown rice syrup
230 ml/1 cup non-dairy milk

For the apple layer
500 g/1 lb. 2 oz. tart apples
40 g/3 tablespoons raisins
¼ teaspoon ground cinnamon
2 tablespoons brown rice syrup
juice of ½ lemon

20 x 30-cm/8 x 12-in. baking pan, well oiled

Makes 12 squares

For the poppy-seed layer, boil the milk and pour it over the remaining ingredients. Mix well and cover until ready to use.

For the tofu layer, crumble the tofu with your fingers. Dilute the arrowroot in a little milk, then whisk together all the ingredients.

For the walnut layer, finely grind the walnuts in a spice mill. Mix with the breadcrumbs and syrup. Boil the milk and pour it over the walnut mixture. Cover until ready to use.

For the apple layer, peel and grate the apples by hand with a grater, or core them and use a food processor to grate them. Combine with the remaining ingredients.

Preheat the oven to 180°C (350°F) Gas 4.

If the sheets of filo/phyllo are bigger than your baking pan, cut them to size. Don't worry if a sheet tears as you can easily patch up any damage – only the top 3 sheets need to stay undamaged.

Place a sheet of filo/phyllo in the baking pan. (Cover the remaining sheets with clingfilm/plastic wrap to prevent them from drying out.) Brush oil lightly over the sheet. Cover with another sheet and oil it. Cover with a third sheet (this one doesn't need oiling). Spread the poppy-seed layer evenly over the top with a spatula. Cover with one sheet, oil lightly and cover with a second sheet. Spread the tofu layer on top. Cover with one sheet, oil lightly and cover with a second sheet. Spread the walnut layer on top (but if the mixture has soaked up all the milk, just sprinkle it). Cover with one sheet, oil lightly and cover with a second sheet. Spread the apple layer on top. Brush a little oil over the remaining 3 undamaged sheets and lay them on top of the pie. Brush a little more oil on the top sheet. Tuck in any pastry or filling sticking out of the pan by pushing a spatula between the pie and the sides of the pan. Use a sharp knife to score 12 squares into the pastry.

Bake in the preheated oven for 45–50 minutes, or until the top turns golden brown and the pie isn't wobbly or soft to the touch. Allow to cool completely (at least 5 hours, or overnight) in the pan before serving. It tastes much better when left to soak up the juices.

If you still haven't heard of this dessert of Turkish origin, you are missing out! Baklava is one of those really sweet desserts that you can't eat a lot of. It's a bit of work to make it, but it can be made in advance and requires only four basic ingredients: filo/phyllo sheets, nuts, sweetener and oil. This allows you to play with different types of nuts and sweeteners and create your favourite baklava without fear of messing up.

healthier baklava rolls

Preheat the oven to 180°C (350°F) Gas 4.

For the syrup, put the syrup and vanilla powder in a saucepan with 560 ml/2½ cups water and heat until boiling. Cut one of the lemons in half, then cut one half into slices and add them to the syrup. Lower the heat, cover and cook for a few minutes. Remove from the heat and stir in the juice and zest of the remaining 1½ lemons. Allow to cool completely.

For the filling, grind the walnuts in a spice mill, then mix well with the remaining ingredients.

Mix 50 ml/¼ cup water with 60 ml/¼ cup of the oil.

Place a sheet of filo/phyllo on a dry work surface with the longer side facing you. (Cover the remaining sheets with clingfilm/plastic wrap to prevent them from drying out.) Brush the oil mixture lightly over the sheet. Cover with another sheet of pastry (this one doesn't need oiling).

Take one-tenth of the filling and spread it lengthwise along the bottom edge of the sheet, leaving a 2-cm/¾-inch edge on each side to prevent the filling from spilling out. Roll the sheet up tightly around the filling and into a nice sausage. Repeat this with the remaining sheets of filo/phyllo and the filling. You should have 10 rolls of baklava. Arrange them snugly in the baking pan. Use a sharp knife to score each roll into 5–6 smaller rolls and brush them with the remaining oil.

Bake in the preheated oven until golden brown. Check if the bottoms of the rolls are baked too before taking the pan out of the oven. Pour the syrup evenly over all the rolls.

Allow to cool completely (at least 2 hours, or overnight) in the pan before serving to allow the baklava to soak up the syrup. It will keep in an airtight container in the fridge for up to 1 week.

100 g/½ cup sunflower oil
600 g/1 lb. 5 oz./20 sheets
of filo/phyllo pastry

For the syrup
390 g/1½ cups agave or pure
maple syrup, or to taste
½ teaspoon bourbon vanilla
powder
2 lemons

For the filling
500 g/4½ cups walnuts
120 g/¾ cup semolina/farina
100 g/½ cup Demerara sugar
1 teaspoon baking powder

*40 x 28-cm/16 x 11-in.
baking pan*

Serves 12

CHAPTER 6

Breads & savoury baking

For breakfast, lunch or dinner – in fact at any time of day – what people most often crave is a piece of bread with their meal. From the simplest, quickest loaf, to a proper focaccia, via other savoury bakes such as corn and tofu pie, and rye and olive-oil crackers, this chapter will inspire you to get creative with your vegan savoury baking.

Many of my friends admire my baking skills because I bake fresh bread for my clients almost every day. But after I shared this recipe with them, the looks of admiration in their eyes faded slightly when they realized how ridiculously easy it is to bake! Honestly, no special skills are required to make this crisp-crusted loaf with a chewy inside. Just follow the recipe and you'll do just fine!

no-knead everyday bread

Preheat the oven to 220°C (425°F) Gas 7.

Sift together the unbleached flour and baking powder, then stir in the wholemeal/whole-wheat flour, oats and salt and mix well.

In a separate bowl, mix together the yogurt, water and oil. Pour into the dry ingredients, mixing vigorously with a wooden spoon until you get a sticky dough with no flour left on the bottom of the bowl. The dough should be easy to spoon. If it's very thick and sticky, add 1–2 more tablespoons sparkling mineral water.

In order to get a nicely shaped loaf, cut a sheet of parchment paper to fit inside the loaf pan without any creases. For the seed mix, combine the oats, caraway seeds and sesame seeds, then sprinkle half over the base of the loaf pan. Spoon the dough into the pan, spread level with a wet spatula and top with the remaining seed mix. Press it gently into the dough with the wet spatula.

Put the bread in the preheated oven, lower the temperature to 200°C (400°F) Gas 6 and bake for 1 hour. Use an oven thermometer if you're not sure about the exact temperature in the oven. If you notice that the top of the bread is browning after 40 minutes, cover with a piece of parchment paper and continue baking.

Remove from the oven, allow to cool in the pan for 10 minutes, then tip the bread out of the pan, peel off the paper and allow to cool completely on a wire rack. This will prevent the bread from absorbing moisture and will keep the crust crisp.

Store the bread wrapped in a kitchen towel in a cool, dry place for up to 5 days.

330 g/2¾ cups unbleached plain/all-purpose flour
2 teaspoons baking powder
60 g/½ cup plain wholemeal/whole-wheat flour
50 g/½ cup fine rolled oats
12 g/1½ teaspoons salt
240 ml/1 cup plain soy yogurt (thinner kind, if available)
225 ml/1 cup sparkling mineral water
2 tablespoons olive oil

For the seed mix
2 tablespoons rolled oats
½ teaspoon caraway seeds
2 tablespoons sesame or other seeds

500-g/1-lb. loaf pan

oven thermometer (optional)

Makes about 8 slices

I tried many different pizza and focaccia dough recipes: with baking powder, the old-fashioned way with fresh yeast, etc., but I got the best results ever when making it as explained in the recipe below. It's true that you need a few hours for the dough to rise, but it's worth every minute! I just do a lot of other stuff while the yeast is working its magic…

herb focaccia

**Pizza and Focaccia Dough
 (page 20)**
**4 teaspoons dried herbs of
 your choice, eg. rosemary,
 oregano (or fennel seeds)**
**1 teaspoon coarse sea salt
 (Himalayan, if available)**

*23 x 30 cm/9 x 12-in. baking
pan, well oiled*

Serves 6

Make the Pizza and Focaccia Dough as described on page 20 and allow to rise for 2½ hours in a warm place.

After 2½ hours, shape the dough to fit the prepared baking pan by gently pressing and pushing it from the middle toward the edges. Make dimples by poking the dough with your fingertips. Drizzle with olive oil, cover and allow to rise again for 2 hours. Do not skip this step as the end result will be a much tougher bread without this second rising.

Preheat the oven to 180°C (350°F) Gas 4.

Sprinkle the dried herbs of your choice and the salt over the dough. Bake in the preheated oven for 20 minutes, or until golden and crisp.

Remove from the oven and allow to cool slightly in the pan before cutting into squares.

Focaccia is great with stews and soups but can also be served on any occasion for which you would serve bread. Focaccia sandwiches are exceptionally popular with my family and friends; I cut one focaccia into 6 equal pieces, then slice each piece in half through the middle. I spread tofu mayo or hummus on the bottom half, top with marinated fried or baked tofu, seitan or tempeh and add as many vegetables, pickles, sprouts and greens as I can fit inside. It's a complete meal in itself – very nutritious and very filling.

It's so easy to make crackers that I sometimes wonder why people spend so much money buying them. All you need is 20 minutes to make a batch that will always be so much healthier and taste exactly as you like! I've reduced the quantity of salt in my crackers to a minimum, since I usually serve them with some kind of spicy spread or dip, but if you plan to eat them as a snack, you can add another ⅛ teaspoon of salt to the dough.

rye and olive-oil crackers

Mix together the flours, seeds, salt and some pepper in a bowl.

In a separate bowl, whisk together the oil, 60 ml/¼ cup water and the syrup to emulsify. Slowly pour into the bowl of dry ingredients, stirring until well combined. The dough should quickly form a ball and shouldn't be sticky. Knead a couple of times, just enough to make sure all the ingredients are evenly distributed. Wrap the dough in clingfilm/plastic wrap and allow to rest at room temperature for 10 minutes. This will make rolling out the dough much easier.

Divide the dough into 3 equal portions.

Preheat the oven to 200°C (400°F) Gas 6.

Place the dough between 2 sheets of parchment paper and use a rolling pin to roll it out very thinly. If you like really crunchy crackers, the dough should be almost paper-thin, but if you like a bit of texture, roll it to your preferred thickness.

Use a knife or a pizza cutter to cut out shapes; squares or rectangles are most practical, as you'll have hardly any leftover dough. Re-roll any trimmings. Transfer the crackers to the prepared baking sheet using a spatula or thin knife. Prick each one a couple of times with a fork.

Bake in the preheated oven for about 4–7 minutes, depending on the thickness of the crackers. Remember that they shouldn't brown, just get slightly golden. They will firm up as they cool, so don't expect them to be cracker-crunchy straight out of the oven!

Allow to cool completely and store in an airtight container for 1–2 weeks.

130 g/¾ cup rye flour
130 g/¾ cup unbleached plain/all-purpose flour
2 tablespoons unhulled sesame seeds
½ teaspoon salt
freshly ground black pepper, to taste
50 g/¼ cup olive oil
1 teaspoon brown rice syrup

baking sheet, lined with parchment paper

Makes about 16

There are so many ways to make cornbread and I realized that many people expect it to be sweet, like cake. This one is not a corn 'cake', even though the texture does resemble cake a little. It's a mild bread that I serve with stews, rich salads or soups. I love to eat it on its own too, as a snack when I travel or go for a day trip to the countryside. For the best results, use finely ground yellow cornmeal and a little coarse cornmeal/polenta for sprinkling – it gives the cornbread a good crust.

25-minute cornbread

200 g/1½ cups fine cornmeal
200 g/1½ cups unbleached
  plain/all-purpose flour
1 teaspoon baking powder
½ teaspoon bicarbonate of/
  baking soda
1 teaspoon salt
450 ml/2 cups plain soy milk
75 ml/⅓ cup sparkling mineral
  water
1 tablespoon apple cider
  vinegar
2 tablespoons brown rice
  syrup or other sweetener
2 tablespoons sunflower oil
2 tablespoons coarse
  cornmeal/polenta

23 x 30 cm/9 x 12-in. baking
  pan, well oiled

Makes 12–15 slices

Preheat the oven to 180°C (350°F) Gas 4.

Sift together the cornmeal, flour, baking powder, bicarbonate of/baking soda and salt.

In a separate bowl, whisk together the milk, water, vinegar, syrup and oil. Pour into the bowl of dry ingredients and combine them to get a smooth batter but do not overmix.

Pour the batter into the prepared baking pan and spread level with a spatula. Sprinkle the coarse cornmeal/polenta over the surface of the bread.

Bake in the preheated oven for 25 minutes, or until the bread starts to turn golden and the corners begin to shrink from the sides of the pan. Be careful not to overbake it!

Allow to cool completely in the pan. Store in an airtight container or wrapped in a kitchen towel for up to 5 days.

Grissini are a great snack and a very popular party food. Why many people are reluctant to make them at home, I really don't know. They're so easy! They can be served on their own, with a dip, with soup – the possibilities are numerous and the enjoyment is guaranteed. When my friend Melani was moving into her new apartment, I tied a portion of long grissini with natural raffia strings and gave her this "bouquet" instead of flowers! Do I need to add that we ate them all right away?

grissini with caraway seeds

Whisk the water, yeast and barley malt together in a small bowl, cover and allow to rest for 15 minutes. The yeast will start to foam slightly while it is resting.

In a separate bowl, mix the flours, cornmeal, salt, caraway seeds and 2 tablespoons of the oil. Add the bubbly yeast mixture and mix until it comes together. Transfer to a lightly floured surface and knead until smooth – about 4 minutes. Place on a prepared baking sheet and, using a silicone spatula, rub oil lightly over the dough. Put in the oven with only the light on and allow to rise for 1 hour.

After 1 hour, preheat the oven to 180°C (350°F) Gas 4.

Take the dough out of the oven and shape it into a flat oval shape. Using a sharp, wide knife, cut the dough into strips 1 cm/ ½ inch wide. Pull and stretch each strip into a long stick. Some strips will be longer and thicker so you'll be able to stretch 2 or 3 grissini out of them. You should get about 20 grissini roughly 35 cm/14 inches long. They puff up a little while baking. I never use a rolling pin to stretch them as that flattens them too much and pushes out the air which results in tough grissini.

Place the stretched grissini back on the prepared baking sheets spaced 7 mm/⅓ inch apart. Brush a little oil over each one and bake in the preheated oven, in batches, for 12–15 minutes, turning the grissini over halfway through baking.

Allow to cool on the baking sheets and store in a sealed bag for about 10 days.

140 ml/⅔ cup lukewarm water
5 g/1 teaspoon active dry yeast (additive-free)
1 teaspoon barley malt or other sweetener
190 g/1½ cups strong unbleached bread flour
30 g/¼ cup strong wholemeal/ whole-wheat bread flour
30 g/¼ cup fine cornmeal
½ teaspoon salt
½ teaspoon caraway seeds
3 tablespoons olive oil

baking sheets, lined with parchment paper

Makes 20 long grissini

This is my version of a recipe that dates way back to the time of the Turkish invasions of the Adriatic coast. Traditionally it was baked as a huge circular pie over coals, but since modern families often have four members or fewer and live in tiny city apartments, a recipe for small pies baked in the oven makes much more sense! It's a great lunch that is light yet satisfying, rich in fibre (from the wholemeal/whole-wheat and rye flours), without any raising agents and filled with vegetables.

soparnik pies with onions and greens

100 g/¾ cup wholemeal/
   whole-wheat flour
65 g/½ cup rye flour
¼ teaspoon salt
2 tablespoons olive oil

For the filling
180 g/6½ oz. tender chard
½ small onion
2 garlic cloves
2 tablespoons olive oil
salt and freshly ground
   black pepper, to taste

Serves 1–2

Preheat the oven to 180°C (350°F) Gas 4.

Mix together the flours and salt, then add the oil and rub it in. Slowly add cold water (up to 55 ml/¼ cup) to get a firm dough that doesn't stick to the work surface when you knead it briefly.

Wrap the dough in clingfilm/plastic wrap and allow to rest at room temperature while you prepare the filling.

For the filling, remove any particularly large and tough stems from the chard. Wash, pat dry with a kitchen towel, and thinly slice. Add a pinch of salt to the chopped chard in a bowl and massage in for a minute, or until it begins to wilt. Pat dry with a kitchen towel again. This way, the pie won't turn out soggy.

Finely chop the onion and garlic and add to the wilted chard together with the oil and season with salt and pepper.

Divide the rested dough in half. Put a sheet of parchment paper down and put one portion of dough on it. Roll out with a rolling pin into a circle about 18 cm/7 inches in diameter. Spoon the filling onto the dough circle, leaving a 1-cm/¼-inch border without filling. Roll out the other portion of dough in the same way, prick with a fork and lay over the filling. Seal the pie by folding over the edge of the dough all the way around the circle and pressing together with your fingers. Crimp into a scalloped edge, if you like.

Slide the pie and paper onto a baking sheet and put in the preheated oven. The raw dough is quite dark but you will notice that the top and bottom will turn golden after 22–24 minutes. At this point, remove the pie from the oven and allow to cool slightly.

Serve warm with some chilled soy yogurt, or cool completely, store in a an airtight container and take anywhere you might need a nutritious light meal!

It's always useful to bake some good-quality snacks in advance and have them stored for emergencies! Homemade snacks are always 150% healthier than anything you can buy in the supermarkets or your local store, so why snack on oily chips, processed and additive-rich pretzels, sticks, etc. when you can make your own tasty bites for the whole family to enjoy?

cracker snacks with black sesame seeds

Put the flour, salt and baking powder in a food processor and pulse to mix. Add the margarine and pulse 6–8 times until the mixture resembles coarse breadcrumbs. Add the syrup and pulse again a couple of times. Gradually add the ice-cold milk or water one tablespoon at a time, pulsing until the mixture just begins to clump together. If you pinch some of the crumbly dough and it holds together, it's ready. If the dough doesn't hold together, add a little more liquid and pulse again. Be careful not to add too much otherwise it will make the crackers tough.

Place the dough on a lightly floured work surface. Knead it just enough to form a ball but do not over-knead it. Shape it into a disc, wrap it in clingfilm/plastic wrap and refrigerate it for at least 1 hour, and up to 2 days. If you're in a hurry you can chill the dough in the freezer for 15 minutes. Allow the dough to rest at room temperature for 5–10 minutes before rolling it out.

Preheat the oven to 180°C (350°F) Gas 4.

Place the dough on a sheet of lightly floured parchment paper, dust with a little flour and roll it out with a rolling pin until 1 mm/ 1/32 inch thick. Use a pastry wheel to cut it into short or long sticks, or you could stamp out shapes with a cookie cutter. Slide the crackers and paper onto a baking sheet. Separate each cracker so they don't stick together during baking.

For the topping, lightly brush each cracker with water and sprinkle the black sesame seeds over the top. Salt lightly.

Bake in the preheated oven for 10 minutes, or until the dough puffs up a little and turns golden. Allow to cool completely on the baking sheet. Store in an airtight container for up to 2 weeks.

260 g/2 cups flour of your choice, or a combination of 2–3 different kinds, if you like, chilled (yes, chilled!)
1/4 teaspoon salt
4 teaspoons baking powder
140 g/1 cup non-hydrogenated margarine, chilled
1 tablespoon brown rice syrup
50 ml/1/4 cup ice-cold plain soy milk or water, or as needed

For the topping
black sesame seeds (or other seeds like sesame, caraway, cumin, dried oregano, dried basil etc.)
coarse sea salt

Makes lots!

This is one of my favourite lunches during pumpkin season, served with a big bowl of salad and a cup of non-dairy yogurt. It's important to roll the dough really thinly to get snails that are slightly crunchy but melt in your mouth. I love to use a small amount of onion in the filling, but you can omit it if you want.

pastry snails with spicy pumpkin filling

180 g/1⅓ cups unbleached
  plain/all-purpose flour
¼ teaspoon salt
3 tablespoons sunflower oil

For the filling
200 g/2 cups grated pumpkin,
  eg. Hokkaido or other
  dense-fleshed pumpkin
½ onion, finely chopped
½ teaspoon tamari soy sauce
2 garlic cloves, crushed
¼ teaspoon salt
1 tablespoon olive oil,
  plus extra for brushing
½ teaspoon ground ginger
1 teaspoon lemon juice
freshly ground black pepper,
  to taste

*baking sheet, lined with
  parchment paper*

Makes 8

Preheat the oven to 180°C (350°F) Gas 4.

Mix together the flour and salt, then add the oil and rub it in. Slowly add cold water (up to 80 ml/⅓ cup) to get a dough that doesn't stick to the work surface when you try to knead it.

Wrap the dough in clingfilm/plastic wrap and allow to rest at room temperature while you prepare the filling.

For the filling, mix together all the ingredients with your hands or a wooden spoon. Divide it into 8 equal portions.

Divide the dough into 4 equal portions. While you are working with one, keep the others wrapped in clingfilm/plastic wrap to prevent them drying out.

Put one portion of dough on a sheet of parchment paper, dust with a little flour and shape the dough into a small log with your hands. Roll it out with a rolling pin, as thinly as you can, into a square. The sheet of dough should be almost see-through. Trim any uneven edges, then cut in half to make 2 equal rectangles. These will make 2 snails.

Spread one portion of filling along the bottom edge of the rectangle. Roll the rectangle up carefully around the filling and into a nice, tight sausage. Bend it into a spiral/snail shape. Seal the edge by wetting your finger and pressing it gently but firmly against the snail. Tuck the end neatly underneath the snail. Repeat with the remaining sheets and filling to get 8 snails.

Arrange the snails on the prepared baking sheet and brush them lightly with oil. Bake in the preheated oven for 35–40 minutes until golden.

Allow to cool slightly (or completely), then serve plain or brushed with a little more oil and soy sauce if you prefer them to be saltier. These snails are great as a portable meal too – very practical!

A vegan version of Greek filo/phyllo pie, this dish makes an excellent lunch or dinner and is very filling. Corn kernels add a nice sweetness and texture to the smooth tofu layers, but using some blanched greens instead of corn is also a delicious variation worth trying. Serve with a big bowl of salad, or a cup of non-dairy yogurt if you're in a hurry.

corn and tofu pie

If using canned corn, wash it and drain well. In a big bowl, crumble the tofu with your fingers and add the corn, oil, salt, milk and hot water and mix until well combined. Whisk in the cornmeal. The filling should be moderately smooth besides the corn and small pieces of tofu.

Preheat the oven to 180°C (350°F) Gas 4.

If the sheets of filo/phyllo are bigger than your baking pan, cut them to size. Don't worry if a sheet tears as you can easily patch up any damage – only the top 2 sheets need to stay undamaged.

Place a sheet of filo/phyllo in the baking pan. (Cover the remaining sheets with clingfilm/plastic wrap to prevent them from drying out.) Brush oil lightly over the sheet. Cover with another sheet and oil it. Repeat this process with 2 more sheets.

Spread one-fifth of the filling evenly over the top with a spatula. Cover with one sheet, oil lightly and cover with a second sheet (this one doesn't need oiling). Spread one-fifth of the filling evenly over the top. Continue like this until you have used up all the filling, and you have 5 layers each of filling and filo/phyllo sheets.

To finish, brush a little oil over the remaining 5 sheets of filo/phyllo and lay them on top of the pie – the 2 best, undamaged sheets should be on the top. Tuck in any pastry or filling sticking out of the pan by pushing a spatula between the pie and the sides of the pan. Use a sharp knife to score 12 squares into the pastry.

Bake in the preheated oven for 45 minutes, or until the top turns golden brown and the pie isn't wobbly or soft to the touch. Allow to cool completely (at least 5 hours, or overnight) in the pan before serving.

500 g/1 lb. 2 oz./17 sheets of filo/phyllo pastry
100 g/½ cup olive oil

For the filling
250 g/2 cups corn kernels, fresh, canned, or frozen and thawed
500 g/1 lb. 2 oz. plain, medium-soft tofu
2 tablespoons olive oil
2¼ teaspoons salt
460 ml/2 cups plain soy milk
230 ml/1 cup hot water
130 g/1 cup fine cornmeal

20 x 30-cm/8 x 12-in. baking pan, well oiled

Serves 6–8

CHAPTER 7

Special baked treats

For desserts, festive feasts and family recipes to hand down through the generations – special baked treats will delight anyone who's lucky enough to try them. These treasured celebratory recipes will stay long in the memory of any guest, vegan or not, and inspire them to bake vegan in their own home.

My mum used to make sweet, baked pancakes a lot when I was a kid and it is still one of my favourite dishes. Today when I make it, I replace the eggs and fresh cheese with tofu and non-dairy cream and it tastes the same, if not better! It's a light dessert but we even eat it instead of lunch – a feast for every kid who prefers sweet food to savoury!

baked, lemon-scented pancakes

For the pancakes, mix the milk and 225 ml/1 cup water in a bowl. Stir in the salt, baking powder and lemon zest. Gradually add the flour, whisking vigorously until smooth. The batter should be thicker than conventional, egg-based pancake batter. Allow to rest for at least 15 minutes.

Heat a heavy-based frying pan and brush a little oil over it. When hot, pour a small ladle of batter into the pan and tilt the pan to spread the batter evenly over the surface. Once the edges start turning golden brown, flip the pancake over and cook until golden on the reverse. Transfer to a plate, re-oil the pan and keep making pancakes in this way until all the batter is used up. Try to make the pancakes quite thin and that should give you 10 pancakes in total.

Preheat the oven to 180°C (350°F) Gas 4.

For the filling, put the tofu, 225 ml/1 cup of the cream, the salt, lemon juice and zest and syrup, to taste, in a food processor and blend until smooth. Mix in the raisins: they give a lovely tangy flavour to this dish, but you can omit them and add a little more syrup, if you wish.

Divide the filling between the pancakes, spreading it over each one. Roll the pancakes up tightly and arrange in the prepared baking pan. Pour the remaining cream evenly over the pancakes and garnish with some lemon zest.

Bake in the preheated oven for 15–20 minutes, until golden. Serve warm or cold.

For the pancakes
340 ml/1½ cups plain soy milk
¼ teaspoon salt
¼ teaspoon baking powder
grated zest of 1 lemon
215 g/1⅔ cups unbleached
    plain/all-purpose flour
coconut or sunflower oil,
    for frying

For the filling
340 g/2 cups plain, firm tofu
685 ml/3 cups thick soy or
    oat cream
a pinch of salt
freshly squeezed juice of
    2 lemons
grated zest of 3 lemons,
    plus extra to garnish
brown rice or agave syrup,
    to taste
30–60 g/¼–½ cup raisins
    (optional)

23 x 30 cm/9 x 12-in. baking
    pan or ovenproof dish, oiled

Serves 4–6

What could be more tempting than soft dough filled with tasty fruit, nuts or chocolate? They are great for breakfast or between meals and they're very practical for kids' (or adults') lunchboxes. I like to keep things simple, so I mostly use homemade jam as a filling, but for special occasions I use a nut-based or melted chocolate filling and shape the dough into pockets, rolls or roses!

pockets and roses with sweet fillings

For the dough
300 g/2⅓ cups strong unbleached bread flour
30 g/¼ cup strong wholemeal/whole-wheat flour
5 g/1 teaspoon active dry yeast (additive-free)
¼ teaspoon salt
a pinch of ground turmeric
150 ml/⅔ cup plain soy milk
40 g/2 tablespoons non-hydrogenated margarine
1 tablespoon sunflower oil
2 tablespoons brown rice syrup, plus extra for brushing

For the filling
180 g/1 full cup toasted hazelnuts, finely ground, or 320 g/1¼ cups naturally sweetened fruit jam
130 g/½ cup brown rice syrup
1 tablespoon carob powder
1–2 tablespoons non-dairy milk, if needed

baking sheet, lined with parchment paper

Makes about 16

For the dough, mix together the flours, yeast, salt and turmeric. Heat the milk in a saucepan until hot, then add the margarine and stir until melted. Add the oil and syrup. Pour into the bowl of dry ingredients and mix with a wooden spoon to get a smooth lump of dough. Transfer to a floured surface and knead vigorously for at least 3 minutes. Place in an oiled bowl, cover with a wet towel and allow to rise for 90 minutes. Punch it down and allow to rise for another 30 minutes.

Preheat the oven to 180°C (350°F) Gas 4.

For the filling, mix the ingredients to get a spreadable paste.

To make 'pockets', roll out the dough on a lightly floured surface until about 2–3 mm/⅛ inch thick and allow to rest like that for 5 minutes. Stamp out as many rounds as you can with a thin glass or cookie cutter about 8.5 cm/3¼ inches in diameter. Re-roll any trimmings and stamp out more rounds.

Place 1 scant tablespoon filling in the middle of each circle. Dip your finger in water and run it around the edge of the pastry round. Fold in half, enclosing the filling, and press the edges together firmly all the way around. Arrange on the prepared baking sheet.

To make 'roses', divide the dough in 3 equal portions. Roll each into a long strip about 2–3 mm/⅛ inch thick, then spread the filling thinly along one long edge. Roll the dough up carefully around the filling and into a sausage. Cut each roll into about 12 slices. Lay on the prepared baking sheet, cut side up.

Bake the 'pockets' or 'roses' in the preheated oven for 15 minutes or until golden. Brush syrup over them while still warm.

These are best eaten the same day but they are still delicious the next 1–2 days. Store in an airtight container.

There is a myth going around that Easter buns are very tricky to make and that you must be an experienced baker to get them right without adding a couple of eggs to the dough. That's why I delayed trying them for a long time, thinking it must be the most difficult thing in the world, but it wasn't. I took my nonna's recipe and after a couple of half-successful tries I got it right. So here's a vegan Easter bun recipe that you can (and should) make throughout the year, not only for Easter!

sugar-free italian easter buns

Mix together the starter ingredients in a mixing bowl, cover and allow to rest for 30 minutes or until doubled in size.

For the dough, mix together the apricots, raisins, rum and orange zest in a bowl and allow to soak while the starter is rising.

Sift together the flour, salt and turmeric in a bowl.

Heat the milk in a saucepan until hot, then add the margarine and stir until melted. Add the vanilla extract and syrup, then the soaked fruit as well as the starter. Mix well. Pour into the flour mix and combine with a wooden spoon to get a smooth lump of dough. Transfer to a floured surface and knead vigorously for at least 5 minutes, until silky and elastic.

Place in an oiled bowl, cover with a wet kitchen towel and allow to rise in a warm spot for 2½ hours or until doubled in size.

Punch down the dough, give it a quick knead, then divide it into three equal portions. Shape each into a ball and put on the prepared baking sheet. Snip V-shaped cuts into the top of each loaf so that they open up during baking. Cover well with a kitchen towel and allow to rise again for 30 minutes or until doubled in size.

Preheat the oven to 200°C (400°F) Gas 6.

Brush a little oil over the buns and bake in the preheated oven for 30–60 minutes or until golden. Brush syrup over them while still hot, then transfer to a wire rack to cool.

These should be stored wrapped in a kitchen towel in a cool and dry place and will keep for a week or a little longer.

sunflower oil, for brushing

For the starter
6 tablespoons plain soy milk, lukewarm
9 g/2 teaspoons active dry yeast (additive-free)
25 g/2 tablespoons rice, pure maple or agave syrup
2 tablespoons strong unbleached bread flour

For the dough
40 g/⅓ cup unsulfured dried apricots, chopped
40 g/⅓ cup raisins
3 tablespoons rum
grated zest of 1 orange
500 g/4 cups strong unbleached bread flour or unbleached spelt flour
½ teaspoon salt
⅛ teaspoon ground turmeric
170 ml/¾ cup plain soy milk
100 g/¾ cup non-hydrogenated margarine
2 teaspoons vanilla extract
65 g/¼ cup rice, pure maple or agave syrup, plus extra for brushing

baking sheet, lined with parchment paper

Makes 3 large buns

These aren't exactly my nonna's crescent rolls, but her old recipe inspired me to make a vegan version since they were a big part of our Christmases. There used to be a giant bowl full of them, carefully rolled in icing/confectioners' sugar, hidden away in one of the cold bedrooms where we (me and my cousins) weren't really allowed to go. But we would steal a couple whenever we could, and hoped nonna wouldn't notice!

my nonna's crescent rolls

For the starter
110 ml/½ cup lukewarm plain soy milk
20 g/½ cube fresh (compressed) yeast
2 tablespoons brown rice syrup

For the dough
400 g/3 cups strong unbleached bread flour
¼ teaspoon bourbon vanilla powder
¼ teaspoon salt
250 g/1⅔ cups non-hydrogenated margarine, at room temperature
2 tablespoons brown rice syrup

For the filling
120 ml/½ cup non-dairy milk
25 g/2 rows of vegan dark/bittersweet chocolate, finely chopped
250 g/2¾ cups finely ground walnuts
5 tablespoons brown rice syrup, plus extra for brushing

baking sheets, lined with parchment paper

Makes about 48

For the starter, whisk the milk, yeast and syrup together in a small bowl, cover and allow to rest for 30 minutes. The yeast will start to foam slightly while it is resting.

For the dough, in a separate bowl, mix together the flour, vanilla and salt, add the margarine and mix in with your fingertips to get a crumbly texture. Add the syrup, mix well, then add the bubbly yeast mixture. Transfer to a lightly floured surface and knead until smooth – about 5 minutes. Shape into a ball and allow to rest at room temperature while you make the filling.

For the filling, heat the milk in a saucepan over medium heat, then add the chocolate and stir until melted. Add the walnuts and syrup and whisk over low heat for 1–2 minutes.

Divide the dough into 4 equal portions.

Put one portion of dough on a sheet of parchment paper. Roll out with a rolling pin into a rough circle about 2 mm/¹⁄₃₂ inch thick. Use a pastry wheel to cut the circle into 12 equal wedges – the circle should now look like a bicycle wheel.

Divide the filling into 48 equal portions – about 1 big teaspoon each. Place a portion of filling horizontally along the base of each dough triangle, then roll up loosely towards the pointed end. Place each roll, point side down, onto a prepared baking sheet. Allow to rest at room temperature for 15 minutes.

Preheat the oven to 180°C (350°F) Gas 4.

Bake the rolls in the preheated oven for 15–20 minutes or until lightly golden. Brush syrup over them while still hot, then transfer to a wire rack to cool. Or roll them in icing/confectioners' sugar if you really, really want to.

Store in an airtight container for a week or a little longer.

The best plums to use here are Italian plums or any small variety that can easily be pitted. You can also use small apricots, frozen plums or even fruit jam as a filling. It's a time-consuming recipe but I never regret a minute spent making it!

plum dumplings

Boil the potatoes in their skins until very tender. Drain, allow to cool a little, then peel. (This is the best way to boil potatoes for dumplings, but if you don't have time, peel them, cut into chunks and boil until very tender.) Mash them well until free of lumps but do not blend them in a food processor otherwise they will turn gluey!

Put the margarine, milk and cream in a small saucepan and heat over low heat until the margarine has melted. Add ¾ teaspoon salt and whisk well. Stir gradually into the mashed potatoes to make a thick mash. Stir in the flour and mix thoroughly.

Turn the dough out onto a floured surface and knead in a little extra flour (up to 130 g/1 cup) until the dough is quite soft but doesn't stick to your hands. It should weigh about 1.15 kg/2½ lb.

Divide it in 4 equal portions and roll each one into a fat sausage. Place on a floured tray and refrigerate for 30 minutes.

Meanwhile, heat the oil in a frying pan, add the breadcrumbs and stir continuously over medium heat until golden brown. Transfer to a large plate and mix in the cinnamon.

Carefully start to slice each plum in half around the pit but don't halve it completely – you just want to remove the pit and leave the plum whole.

Bring a large saucepan of water to a slow boil and add the remaining salt. Preheat the oven to 180°C (350°F) Gas 4.

Take the dough out of the fridge. With your palms, flatten each sausage into a 24 x 8-cm/9½ x 3½-inch strip. Cut each strip into 4 squares. Fill each plum with one teaspoon maple syrup and place on a square, trying not to let the syrup escape. Bring the corners up and around the plum. Pinch the seams together tightly to seal.

Gently drop about 4 dumplings into the pan of boiling water. Once they float to the surface, cook for about 5 minutes. Take out, drain well and roll each dumpling in the breadcrumbs until coated. Cook all the remaining dumplings in this way.

Serve warm with syrup drizzled over them.

800 g/4 medium russet potatoes, scrubbed clean
2 tablespoons non-hydrogenated margarine
75 ml/⅓ cup plain soy milk
40 ml/3 tablespoons soy or oat cream
2¾ teaspoons salt
200 g/1½ cups unbleached plain/all-purpose flour, plus plenty extra for kneading
5 tablespoons sunflower oil
95 g/1 cup fine breadcrumbs
¼ teaspoon ground cinnamon
480 g/16 small plums, eg. Italian prune plums
110 g/16 teaspoons pure maple syrup, plus extra for serving

Makes 16

index

acknowledgments

I'd like to thank:

Lisa Clayton, THE fairy – thanks for being at the right place at the right time and for spreading the word about my cooking adventures!

Ivor Somrak, THE husband – thank you so, so much for your loving words of support, loving hugs, and loving foot massages I needed badly after all the testing I did for this cookbook! Also, for designing me the coolest website ever! www.rentajchefa.com

Nada and Branko, THE parents – growing up surrounded by your art and creativity made me realize how important it is to do what you love, no matter how hard it can sometimes be. Thank you!

Irena and Boris Somrak, THE in-laws – without your love and support I wouldn't have been able to achieve so much in the past couple of years. Thank you for being there for me.

Fumica and Milena, THE grandmas – you both made me fall in love with cooking and baking and I cannot thank you enough for that.

Jadranka and Zlatko Peji – for offering me my first vegan baking job. That opportunity made me realize how much I really loved baking.

Everybody at Ryland Peters & Small – you made this book as beautiful as it is, and Céline Hughes, you are definitely THE commissioning editor!

Ivana and Melani, THE girlfriends – thank you for being there for me for most of my life!

All my other beautiful friends, students, clients and Facebook fans – your support of my work and the daily feedback I get keep me motivated to work even harder! Thank you all!

And last but not least, my dear cat Bu, THE pet – you kept me company during long baking nights and never failed to show interest in what was going on in the oven. Your burnt whiskers are proof of your support of my work!